Professional
Women
at Work

PROFESSIONAL WOMEN AT WORK

Interactions, Tacit Understandings, and the Non-Trivial Nature of Trivia in Bureaucratic Settings

JERRY JACOBS
III

BERGIN & GARVEY

Westport, Connecticut • London

HD6054.2
.U6
J33
1994

Library of Congress Cataloging-in-Publication Data

Jacobs, Jerry.
   Professional women at work : interactions, tacit understandings,
and the non-trivial nature of trivia in bureaucratic settings   /
Jerry Jacobs.
      p. cm.
   Includes bibliographical references and index.
   ISBN 0–89789–380–8 (alk. paper)
   1. Women in the professions—United States—Case studies.
2. Women—Employment—United States—Case studies.   3. Industrial
sociology—United States.   4. Work.   I. Title.
HD6054.2.U6J33   1994
331.4´0973—dc20   93–37848

British Library Cataloguing in Publication Data is available.

Library of Congress Catalog Card Number: 93-37848
ISBN: 0–89789–380–8

First published in 1994

Bergin & Garvey, 88 Post Road West, Westport, CT 06881
An imprint of Greenwood Publishing Group, Inc.

Printed in the United States of America

The paper used in this book complies with the
Permanent Paper Standard issued by the National
Information Standards Organization (Z39.48–1984).

10 9 8 7 6 5 4 3 2 1

Contents

Introduction

We made a trip to the Gulf [of California]. . . . One of the reasons we gave ourselves for this trip—and when we used this reason, we called the trip an expedition—was to observe the distribution of invertebrates, to see and record their kinds and numbers, how they lived together, what they ate, and how they reproduced. That plan was simple, straight-forward, and only part of the truth. But we did tell the truth to ourselves. We were curious. . . . We wanted to see everything our eyes would accommodate, to think what we could, and, out of our seeing and thinking, to build some kind of structure in modeled imitation of the observed reality. We knew that what we would see and record and construct would be warped, as all knowledge patterns are warped. . . . But knowing this, we might not fall into too many holes—we might maintain some balance between our warp and the separate thing, the external reality. . . . For example: the Mexican sierra has "XVII-15-IX" spines in the dorsal fin. These can easily be counted. But if the sierra strikes hard on the line so that our hands are burned, if the fish sounds and nearly escapes and finally comes in over the rail, his colors pulsing and his tail beating the air, a whole new relational externality has come into being—an entity which is more than the sum of the fish plus the fisherman. The only way to count the spines of the sierra unaffected by this second relational reality is to sit in the laboratory, open an evil-smelling jar, remove a stiff colorless fish from formalin solution, count the spines, and write the truth "D.XVII-15-IX." (Steinbeck, 1986: 2–3)

There are many books of the "spine-counting" variety on the sociology of work, but very few that attempt to recapture the experience of catching the fish or that describe in any detail the act of doing so. While both approaches provide descriptions of work that may be accurate and contribute to our understanding, the understandings they provide are very different. This book was written in the hope of compensating not only for the greater number of books taking a quantitative-objective, as opposed to qualitative-subjective, approach to work, but also to increase the number offering rich descriptions of work and the work experience.

•

Professional Women at Work

1

Qualitative vs. Quantitative Studies of Work

THE LACK OF RICH DESCRIPTION

Despite hundreds of books and articles dealing with work that have been written by sociologists and others, surprisingly few provide us with rich descriptions of the work itself. Furthermore, most that do are not by sociologists but come to us in the form of fictionalized accounts. One good example is Orwell's (1933) autobiographical description of the job of *plongeur* (dishwasher):

> The hours were from seven in the morning till two in the afternoon, and from five in the evening till nine—eleven hours; but it was a fourteen-hour day when I washed up for the dining-room. By the ordinary standards of a Paris plongeur, these are exceptionally short hours. The only hardship of life was the fearful heat and stuffiness of these labyrinthine cellars. . . .
>
> I don't remember all our duties, but they included making tea, coffee and chocolate, fetching meals from the kitchen, wines from the cellar and fruit and so forth from the dining-room, slicing bread, making toast, rolling pats of butter, measuring jam, opening milk-cans, counting lumps of sugar, boiling eggs, cooking porridge, pounding ice, grind-

ing coffee—all this for from a hundred to two hundred customers. The kitchen was thirty yards away and the dining-
room sixty or seventy yards. Everything we sent up in the
service lifts had to be covered by a voucher, and the vouch-
ers had to be carefully filed, and there was trouble if even a
lump of sugar was lost. Besides this, we had to supply the
staff with bread and coffee, and fetch the meals for the wait-
ers upstairs. All in all, it was a complicated job.

I calculated that one had to walk and run about fifteen
miles during the day, and yet the strain of the work was more
mental than physical. Nothing could be easier, on the face of
it, than this stupid scullion work, but it is astonishingly hard
when one is in a hurry. One has to leap to and fro between a
multitude of jobs—it is like sorting a pack of cards against the
clock. . . . Mario [a co-worker] said, no doubt truly, that it took
a year to make a reliable cafetier (pp. 61–63).

An excerpt from a more recent work by Wolfe (1987:118–22),
Bonfire of the Vanities, describes a typical day in the life of a judge,
prosecutor, and defense attorney administering bureaucratic jus-
tice in a Bronx, New York, courtroom.

Rich, if more prosaic, accounts are also found in the official documents of Victorian England (Pike, 1972). For example, one report
by a Mr. White describes the kind of work that children did in the
manufacturing of bricks.

Messrs. Bake & Co.'s firebrick works, Brierly Hill: Some girls
and women were engaged in "drawing a kiln," i.e., taking
out the baked bricks. A kiln is sometimes too hot to be
entered at all, and the people are obliged to wait. This was
warm at the door-way, and like an oven inside, where some
stood, the others forming a line to hand or rather toss on the
bricks, two at a time, from one to the other, to a cart outside,
where they were being packed.

A small girl of 12, forming one of the lines, struck me by
the earnest way in which she was doing her share of work
which certainly is heavy for a child, as a slight calculation
shows. The kiln, containing 17,000 bricks, of 7¼ lbs. each
when dry, was to be emptied by ten persons a day and a half;

i.e., this girl had to catch and toss on to her neighbor in a day
of only the usual length a weight of more than 36 tons, and
in so doing to make backwards and forwards 11,333 complete half turns of her body, while raised from the ground on
a sloping plank (pp. 131–32).

Data of this sort, that is, fictional and documentary descriptions,
constitute a potential resource for those interested in what is actually done on the job and how the work is accomplished. They also
help us to see the extent to which the work that is done squares
with formal job descriptions and how the discrepancy between
the two may lead a worker to believe that the job is better or worse
than he or she first supposed. This in turn can help us to understand such important elements of work as job satisfaction and
worker discontent.

If fictional and documentary accounts are useful in the above
regard, planned and well-executed qualitative sociological studies
dealing with the actual accomplishment of work would be even
better. On the other hand, epidemiological studies of risk, safety,
or health hazards on the job; attitudinal surveys; and studies dealing with the formal organization of work offer little assistance to
those who require good descriptions of work. Such descriptions
require, among other things, the extended face-to-face interaction
of the researcher and the researched, both in and out of the work
setting. Quantitative studies usually do not meet this basic
requirement of qualitative research.

In light of this need, the following question arises: How many
and what sorts of qualitative sociological studies that provide good
descriptions of work are available? There are a number of studies
that come to mind. For example, there is Ute's study of a traffic
court and Ponte's of a motor vehicle department (1974); Gubrium's
study of nursing homes (1975); Jacobs's study of a reception and
assessment center in London, England (1982); Friedland and Nelkin's study of migrant workers (1971); Dalton's classic study of *Men
Who Manage* (1966); Hochschild's study of flight attendants (1983);
and Johnson's (1975) and Jacobs's (1969) study of social workers.

It is important to note, however, that while these and other
qualitative studies provide good descriptions of work and work
settings, most are not really studies in the sociology of work per

se. That is, the authors had different topics in mind when they conducted their research, for example, a book on field studies, another on managing emotions, or a paper on bureaucracy. Jacobs (1989) has dealt with the virtue of mining a work on one topic to gain data for the study of another.

While these and a number of other works in this vein might be cited, the fact remains that the number of qualitative studies offering good descriptions of work are minuscule compared to the number of quantitative studies. If we consider only research specifically intended to deal with the sociology of work, the number is very small indeed. One example of the problems associated with placing undue emphasis on quantitative studies of work can be seen with respect to the topic of risk.

QUANTITATIVE STUDIES OF EMPLOYMENT RISK: SOME INHERENT PROBLEMS

The identification of particular aspects of risk to study and the sociological methods used to study them have traditionally been derived from certain political, economic, organizational, and intellectual preferences. In sociology, the intellectual guide has been the methodological orientation of positivism. Organizationally, it has been guided by the needs of industry to study hazardous occupations and occupational practices on the work site. This concern has a political component that is linked inexorably to economic concerns; for example, there are federal, state, and local agencies who monitor the safety of the workplace and determine objectively the extent of risk to which workers are subject. Ignoring these safety guidelines could lead to fines.

Concern with safety has led to numerous studies of objectively determined occupational risk. Many of these are conducted by public health professionals who determine risk as relative risk or as an odds ratio. Fatal occupational injuries of Texas women (Davis, Honchar, and Suarez, 1987); crashes among truck drivers (Stein and Jones, 1988); the relationship between job characteristics and myocardial infarction (Karasek et al., 1988); cancer incidence among cosmetologists (Cantor et al., 1988; Teta et al., 1984); and worker exposure to inorganic arsenate (OSHA, 1983) are some examples of studies of this kind.

In these studies of occupational hazards, the extent of risk to health or life is objectively determined by others who have developed objective and external measures of risk that are understood to operate independently of the degree of risk perceived by the actor. While these studies and others assess occupational risk, they do so by invoking criteria of risk that are established by the researcher, not the subject.

A similar methodological bias occurs in the psychological and business management literature on risk (Cohen, Jaffrey, and Said, 1987; Fagley and Miller, 1987; Hertz and Thomas, 1983; Levin, Snyder, and Chapman, 1988; MacCrimmon and Wehrung, 1986; Steufert, 1986). Studies dealing with self-perceived risk on the job are practically nonexistent. In fact, while a computer search of the literature revealed several hundred references to "risk in education, assessment of, occupations, business, medical and public health," not a single entry emerged under "risk: self-assessment"; "risk: qualitative studies"; or "risk: everyday life." Qualitative studies of risk on the job (or in other settings) that would provide a better description and understanding of self-perceived risk are sorely lacking.

SOME CONSEQUENCES OF AN EMPHASIS ON QUANTITATIVE STUDIES

We have indicated above the prevalence of positivistic sociological studies of risk within the area of mainstream American sociology. There are a number of consequences associated with this methodological preference for studying external objective, rather than internal subjective, phenomena. One has been noted by Tart (1972) in *Science*:

A recent Gallup poll [*Newsweek*, January 25, 1971, p. 25] indicated that approximately half of American college students have tried marijuana, and a large number of them use it fairly regularly. They do this at the risk of having their careers ruined and going to jail for several years. Why? Conventional research on the nature of marijuana intoxication tells us that the primary effects are a slight increase in heart rate, reddening of the eyes, some difficulty with memory,

and small decrements in performance on complex psycho-motor tests.
Would you risk going to jail to experience these?
A young marijuana smoker who hears a scientist or a physician talk about these findings as the basic nature of marijuana intoxication will simply sneer and have his anti-scientific attitude further reinforced. It is clear to him that the scientist has no real understanding of what marijuana intox-ication is all about. [quoted in Schwartz and Jacobs, 1979]

It is argued that quantitative positivistic studies of drug use conducted according to the guidelines of the "scientific method" will necessarily preclude any real understanding of risk or drug use as perceived and experienced by the drug user. This is so since the acquisition of such an understanding would necessitate the researcher including in the research equation the study of the actor's subjective state of mind and the problem of intersubjectiv-ity in the study of the collectivity. These aspects of the human con-dition have traditionally been excluded from quantitative positivistic studies. These exclusionary practices would also pre-clude the possibility of the positivistic researcher studying him or herself if, for example, the researcher was an illicit drug user. This critique of quantitative studies of drug use and abuse applies equally well to the study of work.

A detailed discussion of why positivistic researchers studying employment risk have chosen to by-pass the above resources is beyond the scope of this chapter. As inferred above, one reason involves the positivist's commitment to the scientific method that promises the researcher that, if strictly adhered to and properly applied, scientifically conducted studies produce scientifically valid findings. A commitment to this goal has resulted in most existing studies focusing on the objective external aspects of employment risk. Subjective studies of the actor's self-assessment of risk are rare.

Schwartz and Jacobs (1979) recognized another problem associ-ated with the objective study of subjective phenomena. One exam-ple of this problem is the little voice in our heads that says the words that we read as we read them. Most of us hear this voice in our head speaking the words that we read, as clearly as we could hear the voice of another person reading them aloud to us. In this sense it exists. The problem with scientifically studying such a voice is that it has no mass and it cannot be seen, weighed, or measured by any existing measuring device. In this sense, it does not exist. This little voice, and a variety of other subjective phenomena like it, present the positivistic researcher with a dilemma. The voice is there and a part of the human condition, and as such, it is something sociologists might be interested in studying. However, it is not there objectively speaking, even though it is easily available to each of us for verification. It is for these and other reasons, that positivistically oriented sociologists have chosen to study objective external phenomena that can be more easily retrieved and measured.

Some intellectual, economic, organizational, and political reasons have been presented as to why existing sociological studies dealing with employment risk have been overwhelmingly positivistic in nature. It has been argued that we should take seriously the contention of Thomas and Znaniecki (1928) that "things perceived as real are real in their consequences." For example, high steel workers, who routinely walk along steel beams six or eight inches wide and could possibly fall twenty or thirty stories to their death with one misstep, are, objectively speaking, a group of persons at high risk. However, it is just as clear that high steel workers in the course of doing their job on a day-to-day basis are not preoccupied with the thought that their next step may be their last. In fact, many people in other occupations who are objectively defined at high risk perceive themselves at low risk. A dramatic case in point is prostitutes working during the AIDS epidemic. On the other hand, some people seen by the positivistic researcher to be involved in low risk employment perceive themselves to be at high risk. We will be concerned with cases of this kind and the real-life consequences of perceived risk, or other definitions of the situation held by workers.

THE CASE FOR QUALITATIVE STUDIES

In as much as work is a large part of most people's everyday life, an example of work in everyday life could involve our hypothetical high steel worker. How do we know high steel workers are not concerned about their next step being their last? One answer to this question is that we have all, probably at one time or another, watched (with wonder) high steel workers assembling tall buildings like giant Tinkertoys. What we see is not a worker in a hard hat slowly taking one timid step after another on a narrow beam, as a child might while learning to walk along a fence rail for the first time. Given the danger, high steel workers walk with what seems to be a cavalier indifference.

If casual observation of this sort does not suffice, there is much historical evidence to support the contention that persons in high-risk occupations frequently see themselves at low risk. An account of steel workers in Victorian England is a case in point (Pike, 1972).

> The lower part of the furnace is in the charge of the keepers and the "stocktaker." They prepare the sand, form the moulds, superintend the casting, weigh the pigs [of iron], and remove "the cinder." At casting-time their situation seems full of peril . . . they may be seen skipping about among rivulets of molten metal with more indifference than a tidy housemaid shows to the water with which she is washing the doorstep; and they flit about among sparks and burning fragments of fuel as unconcernedly as a harlequin jumps through a blaze of squibs.
>
> Sometimes, indeed, accidents occur: the sand at the tapping-hole gives way, and the molten metal unexpectedly bursts forth. Or it may happen that the "charge" of the furnace sinks irregularly, arching over, and leaving a hollow such as is often seen at the bottom of an ordinary grate. The vast mass then collapses, and falling suddenly upon the molten cinder, projects it together with no small portion of the blazing contents of the furnace into the "castinghouse." On such occasions, if anyone happened to be standing near, he would be in imminent peril. (pp. 79–80)

The question reduces itself not to *if* but *how* persons whose employment routinely puts them in "imminent peril" can manage a definition of the situation that is opposite to the one held by insurance company statisticians. To address this question, we need to understand that what we see high steel workers doing is a balancing act in more ways than one. High steel workers walking a narrow beam thirty floors up do not consciously consider where to place their left foot or their right at each step of the way in order to maintain their balance. This is what the novice fence walker does and why they frequently fall. High steel workers rarely fall. Somehow they learn to walk beams without thinking. To think about walking beams the way a child thinks about walking a fence would invite disaster. The success of high steel workers in routinely walking narrow beams turns upon their learning to do it without much conscious awareness. Unlike the child, the steel worker's definition of the situation is not that he is about to undertake the risky business of walking a narrow beam and to see if, through care, skill, and luck, he can make it across each time. He simply walks the beam to get to the other side, much as one walks to the store to get a loaf of bread.

On the other hand, he cannot be totally unaware of what he is doing for if he fell, others would say that he was careless or not consciously aware of what he was doing. Balancing acts between little conscious awareness and enough conscious awareness is tricky business and a risky one if one is a high steel worker. How these workers learn to walk beams the way they do, and how this allows them to perceive a risky job as "just a job," ultimately has as much (or more) to do with how risky the job "really is" than how wide the beams are, how often they walk them, or how hard the wind is blowing thirty stories above the ground. In fact, Jones (1984) tells us that high steel work is considered dangerous only under two specific conditions—when it is raining or snowing. Under normal conditions, high steel workers even drink on the job just to keep it interesting. What motivates iron workers to do the work they do? Certainly it is not money alone. In 1950 iron-workers in Montreal made $1.55 per hour. Those in the United States averaged about twice that amount (Jones, 1984).

These and other questions that quantitative sociologists do not entertain or attempt to answer have a great deal to do with what they are concerned with, that is, "risk assessment." There are many reasons for this neglect. Some have been spelled out earlier in this chapter. Others have been dealt with elsewhere (Schwartz and Jacobs, 1979). The conclusion that we can draw is that quantitative sociologists have not neglected these questions by chance.

Their choice in addressing a different set of questions than qualitative sociologists, in an effort to assess the risk of various occupations, is in one sense no choice at all. Nor is it wrong for them to
neglect the questions that qualitative sociologists think are important, since "there's no sin in necessity." They have not dealt with
the kinds of questions proposed by qualitative sociology because
their methodology provides no way to deal with them. By the
same token, they have chosen to address the kinds of questions
they are concerned with because their methods provide a reasonable means of studying questions of this kind. As previously
noted, the net result is that the combined efforts of quantitative
and qualitative studies promise to provide not only more understanding of risk, but different understandings to different sets of
questions.

In short, quantitative and qualitative sociologists interested in
the question of risk assessment are not trying to answer the same
question when they ask, "How much risk is involved in high steel
work?" It is not just that each is using a different set of research
methods, but rather, they are addressing different sets of questions even when they seem to address the same question of risk
assessment.

THE APPLICATION OF QUALITATIVE METHODS

With this formulation of some of the differences between quantitative and qualitative sociological studies of risk, we can now
consider some of the ways in which qualitative sociologists might
try to answer the question of how high steel workers manage to
view a high-risk job as low risk. One previously noted resource
available to qualitative sociologists that is not available to quantitative sociologists, who recommend (in the name of objectivity)
that we study only others, is for the researcher to become a high
steel worker and then study him or herself. Another resource,
short of becoming part of a group under study, is to spend a lot of
time with the group both on and off the job. That is, one can
become a friend or acquaintance of one or more high steel workers
and socialize with them on and off the job. A lot can be learned
from face-to-face encounters of this kind (Jones, 1984). One might
also arrange to spend time on the work site (short of walking

beams), observing high steel workers and interacting with them during coffee and lunch breaks. In addition to these resources, qualitative sociologists can also conduct open-ended interviews with high steel workers after establishing the requisite rapport. These interviews can be used to help construct work biographies and plot and understand careers. Interviews of this kind are different than those sometimes conducted by quantitative sociologists in the following ways. First, quantitative sociologists typically request information from strangers and not persons who have become friends or acquaintances. Second, the questions they ask are structured, which assumes that the quantitative sociologist knows in advance which questions are important to ask and have answered. In comparison, the qualitative sociologist using open-ended interviewing techniques hopes to find, in the course of the interview, not only good answers but good questions. Here it is not assumed that one knows in advance which questions are good and why, although one would have better grounds for such an assumption in qualitative sociology than in quantitative. The reason for this is that before qualitative interviewing begins, a good deal of on-site observation and interaction between the researcher and the researched has already taken place. Each has gotten to know the other and has some basis for assessing which things are important to the other, which are not, and why.

Through the use of these and other qualitative methods, the researcher can reconstruct the social reality of the high steel worker and come to understand why they are able to complete the monumental task they undertake, while most other workers (even those in equally high-risk occupations) would be incapable of even starting them.

We have seen how this means that the worker must come to take his or her job for granted, that is, treat the work nonproblematically. This would mean that high steel workers need to redefine their high-risk job as a low-risk job. We have dealt with some of the things that this entails and how it is accomplished.

In this chapter, quantitative and qualitative studies have been shown to contribute something to our understanding of work. However, the "something" is not the same in both cases. Each methodology constrains us, not only with respect to what we find interesting, or how to go about studying it, but also with respect to what we can hope to find out. Qualitative research studies of work promise to give us not just more data but also different kinds of data than that given from quantitative studies. The prospect exists that such research will help contribute to a stronger understanding of work and the possibility of prediction and control that quantitative and many qualitative sociologists have long hoped for, as well as an enhanced understanding of the experience of work as perceived by the worker. This in turn requires rich biographical data and good descriptive studies of work and workers' self-assessments. The remainder of this book will be devoted to this undertaking.

2

Understanding Work and Workers: A Respect for Trivia and the Need for Rich Description and Subjective Assessments

"And now I'll tell you something, Mr. Detective." She raised her
thin rump from her chair, leaned forward across the desk and fixed
Dalgliesh with her beady eyes. He willed himself to meet them
without blinking and they stared at each other like a couple of
wrestlers before a bout.

"Yes, Miss Collins?"

She stuck a lean nodular finger and prodded him sharply in the
chest. Dalgliesh winced.

"No one had any right to take that bottle out of the lavatory
without my permission or to use it for any other purpose except for
cleaning the lavatory bowl. Nobody!"

It was apparent where in Miss Collins' eyes the full enormity of
the crime had lain. (James, 1989: 132)

In the above quotation from P. D. James's *Shroud for a Nightingale*,
Miss Collins was the cleaning lady at a nurse's training facility,
where a nurse had recently been brutally murdered. She and a
number of other suspects are being interviewed by Chief Inspec-
tor Adam Dalgliesh of Scotland Yard. The murder victim was a
stand-in for a real patient and was inadvertently given a solution
of corrosive disinfectant (toilet cleaner) thought to be milk by
those administering it in the course of demonstrating a medical

procedure. It is obvious to Dalgliesh from the cleaning lady's con-
cluding remarks that she felt that the theft and unauthorized use
of the toilet cleaner was a more serious crime than the murder
itself. How could one explain her seemingly bizarre definition of
the situation, which was at odds not only with the chief inspec-
tor's assessment but also with what one would expect of any normal layperson's understanding of the case? How could such a
trivial offense be elevated to such a high level of significance?

One way to try to understand the cleaning lady's perspective
would be to invoke a number of major rational formal models of
work and workers. For example, Miss Collins was an employee of
a large organization (a hospital). Could we perhaps come to
understand her view by studying the hospital's formal organization chart and her structural relationship to other employees; or,
since she was in charge of the cleaning staff, her managerial techniques; or, by generating a computer model of her ability to provide for the rational and timely distribution of resources necessary
to complete routine cleaning tasks (did she provide her staff with
enough toilet cleaner to do the job when the job was scheduled to
be done); or would perhaps a time-motion study of toilet bowl
cleaning help? These and other considerations of this kind, however, would be of little or no use in understanding why the cleaning lady thought that the theft and unauthorized use of "her"
toilet cleaner was a more significant, and presumably more relevant and important, event than the murder of a fellow employee.
What might help us, though, to understand her perspective is a
nontrivial study of the effects of trivia in the work setting, which
is rarely found in the literature on the sociology of work.

In addition to those outlined in Chapter 1, there is another reason why quantitative studies of work far outnumber qualitative
studies. It was argued toward the end of chapter 1 that qualitative
sociologists have methods for uncovering different aspects of
work than quantitative sociologists and that through the application of these methods they arrive at different understandings of
work. All of this is true. However, this sketch is also a gross over-
simplification of the problems qualitative sociologists face, since
one of their major goals is to get the worker to describe in detail
the work that he or she does. One problem with being able to do
so is inferred in the subtitle of this book; that is, one is not con-

sciously aware of the many aspects of the job that are tacitly understood.

To begin with, for workers to be able to tell the researcher about what they do implies that they are consciously aware of what they do and how they learned to do it. In the earlier example of high steel workers, we saw that workers somehow learned to walk narrow beams high above the ground without giving it much thought. The workers, though, have little conscious awareness of how they learned to walk beams and/or how they came to think of beam walking as just a part of the job and not as a risky feature of the job.

The research problem then becomes, How can the researcher get the worker to address those aspects of the job that the researcher is interested in, but which are (and have been) of little or no conscious concern to the worker? This has been one of the major problems in studying the sociology of everyday life, of which work may be seen as a subset. It is not only the worker who is unaware and/or unconcerned with what he or she sees as the routine, trivial, and inconsequential aspects of his or her job, but he or she finds it difficult to understand why the researcher would be interested in what is viewed as so much trivia. This makes it especially difficult for the worker to retrieve and convey the kind of data that qualitative sociologists are interested in. There are a number of reasons why workers and researchers are indifferent to the routine features of the job.

First, as indicated above, workers typically do not know how they came to know what they know that makes the job doable. Second, they cannot see why they or anyone else would be interested in that question, since it would not change the fact that they have somehow learned what they needed to do the job. Furthermore, they believe that learning about what they learned or how they learned it would in no way change their job performance, job satisfaction, or anything else. Third, the problem is not only that the worker is frequently unable to provide the kinds of information that the qualitative researcher seeks, but that the researcher may be as uninterested in these questions as the worker. This is true not only of quantitative sociologists (who have avoided the kinds of issues and questions posed here) but of many qualitative sociologists as well. There are a number of reasons for this, some of which qualitative and quantitative sociologists share.

First is a notion that one wants to pose and answer "important" questions as opposed to "trivial" ones. Second, there's the notion that the study of trivia leads to the formulation of trivial questions and the discovery of trivial answers. Third, both qualitative and quantitative sociologists tend to subscribe to this belief. The net result is that quantitative sociologists are not concerned with how high steel workers learn to walk beams and how their success or failure relates to the question of risk assessment. This question is avoided by quantitative researchers not only because their methodology precludes any way of studying it, but because the question is viewed as trivial, per se, and unworthy of study even if some way could be found to approach the problem. In this sense, workers and quantitative researchers are in agreement regarding their evaluation of the kinds of questions posed here, that is, "Who cares?" It is not, however, only quantitative sociologists who avoid the study of trivia. Many qualitative sociologists also shun this topic and tend to view research on trivia as trivial. The field's general commitment to this belief helps to account for the small number of qualitative (and quantitative) studies of work in particular and everyday life in general that are concerned with the nontrivial nature of trivia.

This attitude is unfortunate, since most social life is composed of trivia. Indeed, it is unusual when something in our everyday life is experienced as unusual, that is, a nonroutine, problematic, atypical, or a not-taken-for-granted part of our everyday life. Some qualitative sociologists have recognized the importance of studying the nontrivial nature of trivia. The works of such diverse persons as Schutz (1967), Garfinkle (1967), Goffman (1959), Simmel (1950) and Emerson (1970) are some examples. Most qualitative sociologists, however, have, as we have seen, avoided the study of trivia in order to formulate what they believed to be more important questions about social life. This is so not only because the study of trivia is seen by most qualitative (and quantitative) sociologists to lead to trivial questions and answers, but because, even for those who believe otherwise, studying the trivia of everyday life can prove to be a difficult undertaking (Schwartz and Jacobs, 1979). As a result, workers and those studying them tend to address the unusual, atypical, and exceptional aspects of work and leave alone the trivial routine features, which ironically results in the exclusion from their field of study most of what they are trying to understand.

The congruence between workers and those studying them, regarding what is trivial and why, is no accident. As Schutz (1967) and Garfinkle (1967) understood, it is not only laypeople but also scientists who routinely invoke the "natural" as opposed to the "scientific" attitude in their work. Conversely, it is not only social scientists who routinely "theorize" about the nature of everyday life, but laypeople as well. Indeed, it is this theorizing that makes possible "scientific" and "lay" understandings, as well as the everyday life that ensues from these understandings.

An example of how difficult it is in the course of an interview to get workers to address the routine, taken-for-granted features of their job is graphically illustrated in the following excerpt from an interview with a university publications co-ordinator.

> *I*: The thing that I am most interested in is the nitty gritty of everyday work. It's hard to address that because people tend to talk about it abstractly. Like "Well I organize this," or "I edited that." For example, one of the things you have to do is sit down with a document that you have to read and see that it has the right grammar and syntax, that they didn't leave something important out, and so on. How do you do that? What do you need to know to do the work you do?
>
> *Joan*: You do it in one of two ways. You can do it with a pen with a hard copy—if somebody would give you something typewritten, and you'd mark it—I usually use a green pen because the designer puts things in red—talks about how to set things up from a design standpoint. Or, the client would give me a disk and I would put the disk in my computer and I would edit it on the screen. It can be done either way. Sometimes the job is done both ways. Sometimes you might make one pass through by hand and then go in on the disk, either keyboard it in yourself—but at all times we try to get a disk from our client so that we can see it right there in front of us. And those disks will interface with typesetting equipment so it [the document] doesn't have to be re-keyboarded in by a typesetter. What we do on disks will go to typesetting and they'll interface in. They'll format it according to how the

designer tells them—where the spaces should be and the size type. But those disks will interface directly with typesetting, and now our disks will interface directly with Macintosh systems, which means they can lay the pages out on the screen and do desktop publishing and get a laser print, so we can do it either way—sometimes both ways. It depends on the job. And then as we make those corrections, we put all these corrections in, we print it out—we usually then give it back to the client, and they would look at it and say, "Well, you know, these are good corrections, but this isn't really right, you should say this—this really isn't right, but everything else is right." So with those corrections back, we put them in on the disk and then it's ready to go to a designer. The designer sees it next. We prepare a hard copy, typewritten, but it is actually run out on the computer, showing the head sizes—like what is an "A head"—the largest headline size you want, and then progress it down so that they know that this is a subhead of this; those two things are a subhead of that. So you go through and you mark your heads, A, B, C, D, E, so when the designer is now going to figure out how to tell typesetting what size heads to make for this; they're going to know what's a big head, what is the title for a whole page and what are all the subheads under that. So, we go through and do that because we're more familiar with the text than anybody else would be. We've read it more times. And we get that all to the designer—the designer designs the publication. If it's something old that has been done before, they just use the existing boards that were created for the printer, and they create new typesetting copy, and they just paste it down over what was there before. If it's a new publication, the designer decides what kind of type they are going to use, where there's going to be photographs, how many pages there are going to be, how the pages are going to fall— they decide all of that after we're through with the manuscript.

I: Who cranks all of this out? Does the university farm out the printing or do they have . . . ?

Joan: Our typesetting is usually done in-house. We have some people who do typesetting out of house, and we have some printing that is done in-house, but we can't do four-color. We can only do two-color. So if you want something with four-color photographs, the university can't do that so those things get jobbed out to outside printers. Some things stay within our university system. You could have a job that would come to us from a university office. We would do the editing, an in-house designer would do the designing, we'd typeset it in-house, we'd print it in-house, we'd bind it in-house, and it would be delivered by [the] physical plant or by the printing plant. So, there are jobs that stay totally in the university and never go out. But there are also a lot of jobs that we deal with outside. So, then if those corrections come back to us in the form of galleys, if they are being run out in traditional typesetting—you know, just running galleys without it being laid out into pages or page proofs. And then we'll review those and make sure all the corrections are in, show them to the client, the client approves them, they come back to us, as many times as it takes to go back and forth—just the way you would for a manuscript of yours, and then when it's ready to be printed it goes to the printer and the printer sends us a blueprint, which is how the publication is actually going to look. We review that to make sure that everything's there, the photographs are where they're supposed to be, the captions are where they're supposed to be, all the pages are there. You know, the client sometimes would see that—it goes to the printer. Maybe we've got four-color photographs on this and maybe the cover is something new and we're not sure how it's going to work. At that point when the printer is ready to print it, the designer and I go to the printer and we would see what that looks like on the printing press. And they'd bring out proofs, and we'd look at them and we'd say, "No, this is too red, this is too yellow, I don't like the way this looks, it wasn't supposed to be this way," so it would even involve our going to the press to check how things are looking right on the press.

It took a special effort for my informant to talk about her job in this way. Doing all that she described in this transcribed excerpt is not something she routinely thinks of or talks about in order to get the job done. She just does it. When she does talk about what has to be done as part of the process of doing it, it is some particular aspect of the work that is confronting her at the time, her "purpose in hand" (Schutz, 1967), that she addresses and not some abstract process. Being able to know and accomplish the process is an essential part of her job. Being able to describe how she is able to know or accomplish the job is not.

The difficulty in addressing this aspect of work is illustrated above. While Joan was more focused than most, she was still unable to say what it is that publications co-ordinators need to know and be able to do in order to do copyediting. What she described, I already knew. These and many of the other procedures she described can be seen as tools that copyeditors use to copyedit. They also tell us how others are involved in the total production process. They say nothing, however, about the fact that one has to know how to type, spell, become computer literate, have a good formal or intuitive grasp of grammar, be able to look at a computer monitor for hours on end, while words, lines, and paragraphs flash by without getting eye strain, disorientation, and/or headaches or backaches. It says nothing of the fact that copyeditors need to know a lot about a great many topics in order to recognize whether or not the text they are reading makes sense, or whether a particular sentence expressed what the author hoped to express in the best possible way. These skills relate only to the copyediting aspect of the job. As we have seen, publications co-ordinators do more than copyedit. They need to have some artistic appreciation, not only of the text, but also of the layout and color schemes associated with the final product. They must also possess good interactional skills in order to deal with the clients and the many other persons involved in the production process. Finally, they must also be well co-ordinated and highly motivated in order to meet what often seems impossible deadlines. However, none of these taken-for-granted skills, attributes, or abilities were included by Joan in her description of what one needed to know, or be capable of, in order to become a successful copyeditor and publications co-ordinator.

While one can learn a great deal from these and other descriptions about what university publications co-ordinators do, one learns very little about what they know that makes the job doable or how they acquired this work-related knowledge. One needs to separate these two aspects of work for analytical purposes. We can with luck learn about the different aspects of work, the sum total of which comprises the job. Joan gave us a better than average description of the work she does. However, she does not know, or cannot tell us, what skills, beliefs, attributes, or understandings are necessary to accomplish the work she describes, or how, when, or where she might have acquired them. Both sets of data are difficult to come by.

This selective inattention to the trivia of work and everyday life is not restricted to laypeople or to social scientists whose job is to display, describe, and explain social life either through the universal language of numbers or the use of natural language. Others using photographs to display visual images of various aspects of society have also tended to ignore the trivial and mundane aspects of social life. Harper (1990), in reviewing a book entitled *Images of History: Nineteenth and Early Twentieth Century Latin American Photographs as Documents* by Robert M. Levine, notes: "Latin American photographers were entrepreneurial tradespeople who made images for specific markets. There was no market for photographs of social problems or even daily life; thus few photographers . . . photographed problematic or mundane aspects of society."

This statement is consistent with the usual indifference of laypeople and qualitative and quantitative sociologists to the trivia of everyday life. We have already discussed how and why this is so. However, we have also indicated that not everyone subscribes to the contention that the study of trivia in everyday life is inherently trivial. This is true for photographers as well as social scientists. Harper tells us that even among Latin American photographers there was a "small number of individuals with an unusual vision and generally a marginal career [who] photographed problematic or mundane aspects of society." While photographing everyday life may have been unusual in Latin America, there has been a strong tradition of documentary photography that emerged in the United States since the end of the nineteenth century. American photographers, a number of whom became famous for their works, photographed the everyday lives of people in urban slums and in industrial settings, child labor, and the Great Depression. These photographs provide visual images of work settings and work that are as vivid as the word images of George Orwell or the reporters' and inspectors' description of Victorian work settings. As such, they provide a resource for pursuing the first form of rich description discussed earlier in the chapter that is so lacking in the literature of work. The problem is that, with photographs, as with the written word, it was not traditionally social scientists who used photography as a way to visually display and study people at work. More often than not it was photographers who provided these rich historical and social documentaries of the mundane features of work and everyday life. Only recently, a small number of social scientists have accepted the use of video cameras, motion pictures, and still photography as legitimate research tools (Becker, 1981; Jacobs, 1974; Schwartz and Jacobs, 1979). Even among this select group, more has been done to document such things as gender roles in advertising (Goffman, 1979) or detailed micro studies of facial expressions (Ekman, 1965), than the routine features of work or other taken-for-granted aspects of everyday life.

In the following excerpt, Lakoff and Scheer (1984) graphically illustrate how powerful and ubiquitous the trivia of everyday life is and how difficult it is to exclude it not only from everyday life but from science (even by those who have been trained to systematically weed it out).

> In the spring of 1979 we were team-teaching a course. Twice a week, before the class met, we would get together to plan what to do during that meeting. Of course, before we got down to serious business, we'd engage in a little "small talk"—and after awhile, noticed the same topics recurring. How terrible I look today; I have to get a haircut, but can't figure out what kind of a haircut would make me look good/tolerable/less disgusting; I can't find clothes that I like that make me look halfway decent; my breasts are too small; I have to lose weight; so-and-so, who is blond, seems to be having more fun . . . and so on, and so on. Then, after a couple of minutes of this, we'd stop and smile at each other, sheepishly. What drivel, we'd say. Here are two professional women with Ph.D.s, meeting to talk about serious and professional matters, and the best we can do is to get bogged

down in *trivia* [emphasis added] about our looks and our feelings about them! We call ourselves feminists, we'd say ruefully. If anybody else we knew—any of our feminist friends—could just hear this conversation! We felt embarrassed, ashamed of ourselves as women and as scholars.

In the final analysis, laypeople and social scientists can adopt one of two basic positions regarding trivia. They can continue to ignore it and thereby ignore most of what they are attempting to study and/or understand about their own and/or other people's lives, or they can recognize and concede the ubiquitous nature of trivia in everyday life and its importance as a serious topic of study. Social science has a lot to gain and nothing to lose by choosing the second option.

It may be different, however, for laypeople. The reluctance of laypeople to recognize trivia may serve as a useful defense mechanism or positive form of adaptation for dealing with the inhospitality of everyday life. After all, if it is true that trivia permeates most aspects of social life, it would seem to follow that most of us live lives full of trivia. Many experts contend that individuals find the recognition and acceptance of this truth hard to accept. Experiencing life as trivial leads to boredom, alienation, existential dilemmas, midlife crises, blasé attitudes, and other conditions that most of us find very hard to bear. Viewed in this way, the ability of people to ignore or remain oblivious to the role of trivia in their everyday lives may be seen as a blessing in disguise. Many in the social and health sciences, as well in belle lettres, believe this to be true.

Social science's general acceptance of an "ignorance is bliss" approach, however, as it relates to our general indifference to trivia and the role it plays in work and other aspects of our everyday lives, may prove to be misguided. After all, what is it about the routine, trivial, mundane aspects of social life that we find so abhorrent? The answer is not easily found. Many have written about the need for social structure and how societal members find it impossible to live in a random universe. This general belief has helped symbolic interactionists, phenomenologists, and structural-functionalists to account (in different ways, of course) for why people are so obsessed with the need for order. But if many have given their undivided attention to our need for order and our anxiety about living by chance, few have seriously addressed our apparent need to avoid recognizing or dealing with trivia.

What causes this aversion? What's wrong with trivia? Why is it a virtue to be concerned with "important matters" and a vice to be concerned with trivia, that is, "unimportant matters"? We have seen that, according to some, the ability of laypeople to ignore the trivia of everyday life may contribute to their mental health and a more congenial existence. But what about social scientists? How does this belief affect their practices? This question is particularly relevant when we realize that most of everyday life is composed of a series of small unimportant but inter-related matters or things. While any one of these events and/or experiences may be seen as inconsequential, the sum total of all of them constitute our lives. Our lives and the lives of others (constituted in much the same way) may be seen as "group life." The study of group life is often given as a definition of what sociologists do. And yet it seems that this is not what sociologists do, since most would rather walk through fire than concern themselves with trivia—the substance of group life. How did this happen? We have seen that within the social sciences important things are seen as consequential and consequential things as meaningful. Unimportant things are seen as inconsequential and inconsequential things as irrelevant or meaningless. It is further understood that it is not the job of social science to study meaningless issues or the issue of meaninglessness. This, as the old joke goes, is the business of philosophy. All of this has contributed in different ways to the aversion of the social sciences to the study of trivia.

The remainder of this book deals with the nontrivial nature of trivia as it relates to the question of work, and what one must know and be capable of in order to make different kinds of work possible.

3

Office Work:
Joan, Publications Co-ordinator

When first I passed by there, it was just an ordinary office with desks and typewriters and filing cabinets and telephones. There were a half a dozen women working there, but there was nothing to distinguish them from millions of other office workers across America, and none of them were pretty.

The men who worked in the office were all about middle age and they did not show any sign of ever having been handsome in their youth or actually anything in their youth. They all looked like people whose names you forget.

They did what they had to do in the office. There was no sign on the window or above the door telling what the office was about, so I never knew what those people were doing. Perhaps they were a division of a large business that was located someplace else.

The people all seemed to know what they were doing, and so I let it go at that, passing by there twice a day: on my way to work and on my way home from work.

A year or so passed and the office remained constant. The people were the same and a certain amount of activity went on: just another little place in the universe. (Brautigan, 1972:68)

This chapter provides a case study analysis of a biography of work based on a transcribed interview with Joan, a publications

co-ordinator in a mid-sized eastern university. An excerpt from
this transcript appeared in Chapter 2. The analysis will deal with
her career development, its motivation, how her prior and newly
learned skills helped her succeed, how her new boss and his
restructuring of the office helped Joan to become upwardly
mobile, the way in which her career line developed, the morale
and interactional problems that the reorganization produced during and after the transition period, and the details of what her job
actually entailed. We will also see how and why Joan's job satisfaction level increased markedly in the university setting, even
though the work she did was essentially the same as what she did
in a variety of other settings when her morale and job satisfaction
were low. In conclusion, an insider's perspective of the life-world
of an office worker is provided through the use of detailed biographical material. The definition of biographical material is as
follows:

> Nothing mysterious is meant by the notion of *biography*.
> Literally, it refers to the events and their meanings . . . that
> make up a person's life. Biography consists of the infinitely
> variable circumstances and events, as well as their chang-
> ing meanings, that constitute the "career" of people. . . .
> These individually unique and incredibly varied experi-
> ences and meanings are part of what it means to be situated
> in a complex social structure. People are situated simulta-
> neously in many "places"—that is, in terms of such factors
> as race, sex, religion, socioeconomic status, and age, among
> others. Being situated in these "places" means that people
> who are similarly situated will experience *roughly* similar
> events, while those located in different "places" within the
> social structure are likely to have correspondingly different
> experiences. . . .
>   It is important to recognize that biography, as used here,
> has no final form. A person has no definitive biography.
> *Biography is constantly in the making; it is constantly being added*
> *to and "remade" as a result of every unique experience and each*
> *new situation.* (Pfuhl, 1986:24)

CAREER PATH

Joan's involvement with office work spanned a period of twenty-seven years—the last seven with the university. She worked in the office of a small pharmaceutical company, a family-owned business, and a major corporation, all in the same city. The first three jobs left her feeling that she was "getting nowhere." A major event precipitating her move to the university occurred when she returned for the second time to the corporate world after an absence of many years. She put it this way:

> When I went back [for the second time to the corporation job], I just thought it was a time warp—twenty years had passed—and I thought, "I can't do this. I can't work here," just because it was the same place. And that's when I started applying at the university and when I got the job.

In 1982 she joined the department of sociology at grade 18 and a salary of $9,000 per year. After about a year the departmental administrative secretary left, and Joan applied for and was given her job. This resulted in a promotion and increase in salary. Three years later, Joan moved to a new position within the university system: publications specialist, grade 20, at a salary of $14,000 per year. In publications, she quickly moved up the career ladder and within the next four years became a publications co-ordinator, grade 45, at a salary of $21,000 per year.

In addition to a series of rapid rank and salary advancements, her benefits increased substantially, as well. On achieving grade 45, she moved from "non-exempt" to "exempt" employee status. This doubled her vacation time from two weeks to one month per year, gained her the same retirement plan that the professional employees had (previously, she had only a noncontributory university retirement program), allowed her more "flex time" to take university tuition-free classes toward her bachelor's degree, and finally, she was no longer required to "count her sick time."

Apart from the economic, status, and educational gains that accrued, there were a number of equally important gains that fell under the general heading of social benefits and job satisfaction. These will be dealt with later.

Notwithstanding all this good news, life in the publications office was not perfect, and there was a downside to all of these career gains. We will see how the career development (or lack of it) of others who worked in publications sometimes enhanced and sometimes hindered Joan's own career. These aspects of office life will also be discussed later.

MOTIVATIONS AND INCENTIVES FOR CAREER CHANGES: "PUSH AND PULL ARE WRITTEN ON THE DOOR OF SUCCESS" (AYALTI, 1971)

As previously noted, Joan's career in office work spanned some twenty-seven years and could be seen either as a failure or a success, depending on the time interval. While she characterized the first twenty years as "going nowhere," the last seven she viewed as a success story.

> *Joan*: Well, when I made the [career] move to exempt from a nonexempt [employment status], I think I was making around $14,000. And when I moved to exempt, it was [raised to] around $16,000. It was quite a jump. And then, in the last few years, I've gotten not a huge raise, but more of a percentage than anyone else in the office. So now, I'm at $21,000. So, that's high for this campus. That's a good salary.
>
> *I*: That's a big jump from where you were.
>
> *Joan*: Yes, it certainly is, because it was seven years ago when I came to the university and I was making under $9,000 per year.

What prompted this abrupt shift from "going nowhere" to "getting someplace"? Actually, there were a number of things that contributed to this change of events. Let's consider some of them in terms of push-pull factors. First the push factors. Twenty years of "going nowhere"—typing, filing, and doing budgets and payrolls in three different office settings—could be seen in any rational model of social action as a push factor. But if the rational push factor is fairly obvious, the pull factors are not. For example, one major consideration that can motivate a career move is the prospect that the change will result in a vertical economic and/or promotional shift. Failing a vertical gain, one would anticipate a horizontal move motivated by the prospect of greater job satisfaction. Neither of these, however, were true in Joan's case. Not only did she not get a salary increase when she accepted the position with the sociology department, but she actually took a cut in pay. Furthermore, the new job was essentially what she had been doing for the past twenty years and provided no increase in intrinsic rewards.

At the time that Joan accepted her university secretarial job, she was a single parent with a teenaged daughter. She knew that after three years on the job, one of the benefits the university provided was free tuition for herself and/or her child. The prospect of a single parent with very limited means getting a free undergraduate education for his or her child at a major university (then worth approximately $40,000) could certainly be counted in the pull column of any rational model of human behavior. This, however, was not a consideration for Joan when she took the job. Rather, she took the position in order to further her own educational goals, not her daughter's. In short, half of what one would have expected in terms of a rational motivational model happened; half didn't. Joan had this to say about the prospect of free tuition as a pull factor:

> *I*: Is one of the things that got you interested in a university job, the fact that your daughter could get a free education?
> *Joan*: No. I came to work here because I wanted to complete my degree. I had been going to university college [a branch of the university giving evening classes for working people pursuing a degree and/or for nonmatriculated students] at night and paying my own way. I thought it [the university] would be a nice place to work and take more and more classes, and I decided that in spite of the low pay, that the tuition benefits [for her] would be worth it. So, I came here [to work] for my own education and having my daughter go was really just a windfall. I never even thought about that [when she applied for the job].

If many of the usual pull factors did not motivate Joan to accept a full-time secretarial position with the university as a nonexempt employee, with two weeks vacation, earning $9,000 a year, what did? One major pull factor was that the university allowed Joan to work and pursue a degree at the same time. Given her limited financial resources and strong motivation, the prospect of free tuition and greater flex time helped pull Joan into her university job. There were, however, other equally strong pull factors, none of which had to do with promotional prospects, salary increases, or enhanced benefits. These factors were generally unofficial fringe benefits and were related to Joan's nonwork-related background. Her strong interest in taking classes and acquiring a university degree had to do in part with her love of literature and her position as a published author. Because of this background, she sought the "invigorating atmosphere" of the university as opposed to the stilted atmosphere of the office jobs she had known in large corporations and small businesses.

> *Joan*: It was for my own educational benefits [that she took the university job]. I knew being on campus would be invigorating. It would be something that you could go to a lecture on your lunch hour and catch something [cultural] after work. You know, there's always somebody reading literature, there's always somebody giving a lecture, always somebody doing something interesting on campus—a million things you could do every week. And these were the kinds of things that I missed working in business and in small places.

One may think, "I understand how fringe benefits may have been a major pull factor in Joan's accepting a university job, but what about her recent rise through the ranks, her promotions, salary increases, shift from nonexempt to exempt status, her daughter's free undergraduate education and her new-found retirement benefits? Aren't these all major pull factors as well?" The answer is yes, they are now, but they were not when Joan accepted her university job in 1982. At that time, the major lure was the prospect of a free education and an invigorating intellectual atmosphere. That these were enticing benefits should come as no surprise. After all, university secretarial positions typically promised neither high salaries nor rapid advancement. It is easily documented that Joan's climb up the career ladder was not a taken-for-granted feature of campus-based office work. We have only to trace the career development of some of the other employees in the publications office to see that upward mobility was for most a slow and painful process.

For example, when Joan first began working in publications, she was a grade 20, and her immediate superior was a grade 45. Four years later, Joan moved from grade 20 to 45, while her boss remained at the same level. Worse still, at that time Joan asked the director if she could be the co-ordinator of a project dealing with the preparation of course catalogs, but he decided to fill that position with someone from outside the office. The outsider became Joan's self-appointed supervisor who delegated the task to Joan. Four years later, with the reorganization of the office by a new director, Joan's former supervisor once again was placed in charge of course catalogs, a job she officially held four years ago. This represented for her not only a lack of upward mobility but a perceived reduction in status.

Another employee who is currently a grade 20 editor was also unhappy about his rate of advancement. Joan described it this way:

> There's also a fellow that works with me a lot of times. He is a copyeditor and perceives that his life is to always be an underling. He can't understand why he never gets promoted because he's been there over two years and "if you're there two years, you should get promoted." And, it's very difficult to explain to him that people don't get promoted that way in the university. Nobody says, "If you're here a year, you get promoted." Sometimes that happens and sometimes it doesn't. So, he has the feeling that "I'm doing the same job as everyone else, why am I not getting grade 45 pay and benefits . . . ?"

If, as we have seen, promotions and raises are hard to come by within the university system, how can we account for Joan's recent success? This is an interesting issue in light of her twenty years of "going nowhere." There are at least four basic dimensions to this question.

DIMENSIONS OF CAREER DEVELOPMENT

Hard Work

What would motivate one to work hard in a rational model of behavior? There are a number of possible answers. For example, exchange theory would predict that someone who felt that his or her work was being appreciated and/or financially rewarded might reciprocate in kind and work harder to show a return of appreciation. The starting salary of Joan's first university job as secretary in the sociology department paid just under $9,000 a year for a full-time job with minimal benefits. This level of financial reward would lead one to predict only sloth. How about the feeling that one's efforts on the job are being appreciated? While Joan did not address this issue directly in our interview, her omission of any mention of how much she enjoyed her job while in the sociology department, or how much they appreciated her, was telling. This was supported by other unobtrusive indicators. For example, Joan's salary rose from just under $9,000 to about $12,500 per year during her stay in the sociology department (a raise of about $3,500 in a three-year period). It escalated from about $13,500 to $21,000 in the next four years (a raise of about $7,500). This means that Joan's salary increases averaged over $700 per year more when she was with the publications office than when she was with the sociology department. This in turn translates into salary increases that were a whopping 40–50 percent higher during the last four years or after her switch to publications.

In short, while Joan's salary increased at a much faster rate in the last four years than in the first three, her rate of growth within the university's system was always above average. One can conclude from this that Joan was always a hard worker, but that she worked harder in publications than in sociology. We will see that how long and how hard Joan worked were directly related to her employer's level of appreciation. This she measured in terms of salary increases, promotions, and higher levels of responsibility.

Another important noneconomic consideration was the diversity of the work. She enjoyed doing different kinds of work that enabled her to learn new skills, as opposed to routine repetitive jobs she could easily do with old skills. The latter she found boring. In brief, Joan liked diversity, learning, challenge, increased responsibility, and autonomy, and she was willing to work long and hard to achieve these goals. In as much as her job in publications provided more of these economic and noneconomic job opportunities and rewards, Joan worked harder in her second position than in her first. Some indication of her industry and dedication can be seen in the following excerpt:

> *Joan*: I usually get there about 7:30 to quarter of eight. I get there early and the office starts at 8:30, so I'm usually the first one in the office. So when I get there it's always quiet. I put on the coffee, I go to my office. Either I clean up what was on my desk from the day before or—I usually make up a list the day before—things that I absolutely have to do the next day. I look at that and I start going through things that I know I have to do before it gets too busy and there are too many people around. . . . Generally, I try to do memos or things that need kind of quiet time when I first get in in the morning . . . and I usually don't leave until 5:30 or 6:00.

Given that the official work hours for the publications office were 8:30 A.M. to 5:00 P.M., Joan typically put in an hour and a half to two hours a day gratis (about eight to ten hours a week).

> *I*: So, is it fair to say that with the promotions and everything, the good news is that you have higher status, better benefits and pay and that you enjoy the kind of work you now do more than before but that you're working more than before?
> *Joan*: Yeah, I'm working a lot more than I worked before. I always work hard, but I'm working harder now [and] longer hours.

Working harder and longer hours gratis was largely motivated by the recognition that the new director accorded Joan. This she saw as related not only to her past performance, but to her future prospects. She put it this way:

> I also see that somehow, with a new boss [the new director] that there's that potential for maybe even another move up the ladder within my own department because now there's talk of a middle management [position being created] which we never had before. So, then there's that potential that instead of being one of the editors, I can be the manager of editors, or a project manager within editors, co-ordinating everybody's job, making sure of who is doing what.

To be eligible for this position, Joan requires only a one-step promotion from grade 45 to 46 and is working hard to achieve it.

Skills

In the previous chapter mention was made of some of the relevant skills Joan required to be able to do her everyday tasks. It was also pointed out that when she described the routine features of her job and how they were accomplished, she totally omitted these taken-for-granted skills from her description. We have seen why these aspects of work are typically omitted by those describing their work-a-day world. For example, Joan did not mention that in order to do the work of a publications co-ordinator (a major component of which was copyediting) one must first learn to spell (good writers may be bad spellers), type, become computer literate, have a good formal or intuitive grasp of grammar and syntax, and be able to look at a computer monitor for hours at a time without suffering the debilitating effects of eye strain, disorientation, headaches, or backaches. An additional requirement is that copyeditors know about a wide range of topics in order to recognize whether or not the text they are copyediting makes any sense, or whether a particular sentence expresses what the author hoped to express in the best, or at least reasonable, way. They also need to have some artistic appreciation, not only of texts, but of layout and color schemes associated with the final product. They must possess good interactional skills in order to deal with clients and other people involved in one way or another with the production process and final outcome. Finally, publications co-ordinators must be motivated and well co-ordinated themselves, in order to be able to co-ordinate others to meet what often seems impossible deadlines. While Joan did not include any of these skills in her job description, they are all prerequisites for successfully completing the kinds of work that she describes. Let's consider some of these relevant skills and where and when she might have acquired them.

A basic skill required of all secretaries is typing. Where and when did Joan learn to type? Joan never revealed when, how, or under what circumstances she first learned to type, but with respect to the needs of her current job, it is obvious that twenty years of secretarial office work would have honed her typing skills to a fine edge. If "practice makes perfect" she must have been at least a competent typist by the time she accepted her first secretarial position with the university in 1982. It was at this time that she also gained some proficiency as a word processor. Finally, much of what she learned on previous jobs were the same tasks required of her by the sociology department and later by the publications office. In describing her job when she first joined publications, she tells us:

> I did budgets. I handled anything having to do with pay. Anything for the department. Like I ordered supplies . . . anything to do with running the office. At that time there were three of us working in the office, so that wasn't a big job [difficult or challenging]. It involved doing payroll, keeping track of people's hours, and recording that. [It also required organizing and filing] . . . And there were many boxes of university publications dating back to the sixties [that] were in boxes and no one had ever put them together in any kind of order, and for months I worked on that—organizing them into an archives file. . . . [And another part of the job] was getting things together for conferences.

These tasks, that is, preparing budgets, payrolls, ordering supplies, and filing and organizing materials, were all skills she had previously learned primarily through "on-the-job training" and lots of "hands-on experience." There was very little formal training. In keeping with this "do-it-yourself" learning process, she is now acquiring the artistic appreciation necessary to recognize acceptable layouts and graphics through her involvement in university art classes.

The Effect of High-Tech Office Equipment on Worker Skill and Competence

If one could osmose or "pick up" filing, typing, bookkeeping and other office skills through years of hands-on experience, one could also learn to spell through on-the-job training, slowly, informally, painfully, and through a process of trial and error, repetition, and recognition. At least all of this was true in the days before high-tech office equipment. Until recently, if one did not learn to type, spell, keep books, or file, one's lack of skills and performance soon came to an employer's attention, and one "found another line of work." Radical changes in office technology, however, have changed all of that. Not withstanding the apparent contradiction, high-level technology has managed to maintain or even increase productivity, while at the same time to reduce the general level of competence among office workers.

How was this sleight of hand possible? In the current scenario, the worker is no longer obliged to type at a typewriter where an error meant an error on the typed page, as well as on the carbon copy, all of which entailed a long and frustrating process of correction. In this scenario, the time, effort, and frustration that correcting errors entailed encouraged one to make as few errors as possible in the first place. The way to avoid errors in the first place was to become a competent typist. The word processor changed all that. An error in hitting a key no longer meant a lengthy and tedious process of correcting two typed copies. The typo no longer appeared on the hard copy at all. By the same token, leaving out a word or line while typing no longer meant retyping the whole page. Misspelled words no longer meant looking up the correct spelling in the dictionary and correcting the errors on the typed page. The computer's built-in dictionary now scans the manuscript for spelling errors, advises the typist of the error, gives the correct spelling, and requires only that the typist insert the correct spelling before instructing the printer to produce the hard copy.

Through the wizardry of the computer, secretaries can also insert or delete letters, words, lines, or paragraphs or move them anywhere throughout the text.

While the machine's capabilities enhance the level of productivity and make the production of clean hard copies easier for the worker to produce, it does not encourage the office worker to become a competent speller, typist, or writer, or to look for and recognize errors. In fact, the computer exhibits these particular features. While it is totally unforgiving if a wrong command is given, it is all-forgiving of the user who produces innumerable errors in the reproduction of the text, in the sense that it makes errors easy to recognize and correct by a competent user. This means that the competence a secretary has to develop has shifted. He or she now has to become proficient primarily in understanding what the computer is capable of doing and how to make it perform these operations. The downside is that the more competent one becomes in operating the computer, the less competent one needs to be in order to accomplish what the typist formerly did. These skills are no longer necessary since the computer is now capable of doing most of them. This reduces not only the motivation to acquire these skills, but it may actually reduce one's existing level of competence. The following is a quote from a woman with fifteen years of office experience (Garson, 1988):

> You can type so fast now, you fly with these new machines. But what it looks like before you correct it! . . . So, what I do, when I'm halfway through something, let's say I did a rough draft but didn't have a chance to edit it or run the spell check—*I used to be a perfect speller before I got this thing* [her computer] [emphasis added]. I'd be so embarrassed to have someone see it. [So, she made sure her boss didn't see it before the corrections were made.]

The net result is that computers and copy machines have made office work easier, faster, and in Weberian terms, more rational (efficient). However, it has simultaneously reduced the worker's need to develop the skills formerly necessary to be considered a good secretary, copyeditor, typist, or bookkeeper. Electronic dictionaries, thesauri, spreadsheets, and copiers, have inadvertently produced a growing pool of incompetent office workers who no longer see the need to develop the skills of reading, writing and arithmetic, since the machines can now deal with these formerly all-important, but now secondary, concerns. The office worker now has only one major "purpose at hand" (Schutz, 1967) and that is to become a skillful operator of the machine that can do most of the things that were formerly required of the operator.

On the societal level, this has led to a number of ironic and dysfunctional circumstances that have recently taken on the scope and stature of social problems. Many high school students don't know their multiplication tables or understand fractions or percents. Recent national math achievement test scores bear this out. Everything from tiny inexpensive handheld calculators to home computers are believed to have contributed to this unhappy state of affairs. The same is true with English composition and reading comprehension. National achievement scores have dropped in these areas as well. While a conclusive cause-and-effect link might be difficult to establish, it seems clear that there is an inverse relationship between the increasing levels of technology and their public acceptance, consumption, and use and national achievement test scores in our public schools. One study indicates that the average number of words in the written vocabulary of children six to fourteen has decreased from 25,000 in 1945 to 10,000 in 1990 (Rinsland, 1990). The consequences of this trend for those entering the workforce, and for the country at large, has been dramatic: "The Labor Secretary's Commission on Achieving Necessary Skills found that 60 percent of Americans between the ages of 21 and 25 lack the basic reading and writing skills needed in the modern work place" (Greenhouse, 1992).

What has all of this to do with Joan's level of office skill and/or her career development? Since Joan loves language, she willingly pursued both reading and writing on and off the job. This, as we have seen, is contrary to the current national trend in learning. Fewer and fewer office personnel have, or desire to have, Joan's literary skills. Why would they? They no longer need the skills they once did to do most office work, and such skills are no longer either recognized or rewarded as they once were (Mills, 1956; Braverman, 1974; and Garson, 1988). A skillful word processor can now get by as well or better than what was once called a "good secretary"—someone who was a competent speller and typist; understood grammar, syntax, and math; and had good interpersonal skills and a sense of personal and company loyalty. While one might show a general indifference to these skills with respect to routine low-level office work, one cannot ignore them if one ever hopes to achieve a more responsible and rewarding job. Such jobs require the kinds of skills that Joan has and fewer and fewer office workers possess because of their myopic view of what it takes to succeed. This leads to a prediction that the path to upward mobility will be slower for the next generation of office workers than it was for Joan because fewer of them will have the requisite skills necessary to move up the career ladder. If the need to advance people is systemic, and the rate of advancement and the percent of those advancing remains constant, those who are advanced will be less competent, by and large, than those who preceded them. The net result on a national level promises bad news on a scale that few can now anticipate.

The introduction of high technology into office work, or our everyday life, has not necessarily made it more difficult or impossible for people to learn, or learn things worth knowing. There has always been and will continue to be people who want to learn and who like diversity, adversity, and challenge. For these people, technological advances will probably make learning easier, not harder. Not everyone, however, is motivated by the intrinsic benefits and rewards of learning. Most seek the more pragmatic goal of acquiring immediate benefits of the greatest magnitude, in the least time, and with the least effort. This has led to the 1980s philosophy of "I want mine, I want it all, and I want it now." We have seen where this approach has left the industrial base of the nation and where it seems to be driving the collective knowledge base.

Joan, who seeks to achieve many of the same financial goals and benefits as her co-workers, has a much better chance of succeeding than they do. Their "rational" pursuit of goals—their nearsighted and instrumental pursuit of short-term, large-scale, low-effort gains—will likely impede their progress. "Getting ahead" ultimately requires the acquisition of skills that now seem to many short-sighted workers as "lacking in relevance" or "a waste of time," skills for which, in the world of work, there seems to be no obvious application or immediate reward. Such an approach to the acquisition of skills and knowledge does not bode well for either the individual or society.

Temperament

While there are many definitions for the word *temperament*, the one most applicable here is "one's customary frame of mind or natural disposition" (Webster, 1982). Joan's frame of mind and natural disposition toward work when she first arrived at the university can be characterized as follows: She believed in working hard, had a positive attitude toward work (most of the time), took a far-sighted approach to gaining recognition and advancement, sought out jobs that were more difficult (if they also provided the prospect of variety, greater autonomy, and the possibility of acquiring new skills), believed in getting work done on time and doing it right, worked at developing good interpersonal skills, and, having spent the last twenty years "getting nowhere," was anxious to complete her college degree and become upwardly mobile. All of these attitudes toward work, in conjunction with the need for change, worked at this juncture in her career to move Joan ahead—faster in the second campus job than in the first, but at a better than average clip in both. We have seen how these life circumstances, and the attitudes toward work that they helped to generate, motivated her to attempt and succeed at achieving upward mobility.

Other factors, however, contributed to this success story. Desperate circumstances (the need for a change, for example) often generate desperate measures. In Joan's case, it took the form of escalated levels of risk taking. It should be noted that prior to her existential crisis, Joan was not a risk taker. But when she applied for the promotion in publications and was turned down, Joan did not do what she would have previously done and passively accept it. Instead, she surprised herself (and her boss) by applying for another campus job that she felt promised better potential. When she found that she was a serious candidate, she informed her boss. This led to a promotion, a substantial salary increase, a change in employment status from nonexempt to exempt, and to a sharp rise in benefits. Joan described her uncharacteristic risk taking this way:

Needless to say, it [being denied a promotion] was not a pleasant experience and at that point I started applying for jobs at other places in the university. I got an interview at University College in the Public Relations Office and it boiled down to the search committee interviewing two [final] candidates [Joan and one other]. When I went to my boss I knew I was being interviewed and I was very much at the end of that process, and that it was going to be 50–50, either I got the job or I didn't at University College. He [the boss] then decided there was probably another opening in our office at a grade 45—and he offered me the job to stay at a higher grade.

Luck

Luck also played a role in Joan's recent career advancement. While working in the sociology department, the administrative secretary left, leaving an opening for Joan to fill. Then, while in the publications office, the old director left. The new one made room for Joan's advancement by restructuring the office and by recognizing Joan's potential to a greater extent than his predecessor. Of course, these lucky breaks would have all come to nothing if Joan had not taken advantage of them. The initiative necessary to do so was generated, at least in part, by the existential crisis noted earlier.

The above circumstances might be characterized by the adage "one thing leads to another." What I've tried to show was which things led to which, when, and why, and how they all affected Joan's career line.

THE WORK OF A PUBLICATIONS CO-ORDINATOR

When Joan moved from the sociology department to publications, what did she think the job of publications specialist would be?

I: Did you have an official job description like you can find on any bulletin board?
Joan: Uh-huh.

I: What did it read like?

Joan: It [the job] was called a "publications specialist." All the jobs [as she later found out] are classified according to publications even though you may not actually work on a publication as an editor, writer, or designer. Even the person who runs the office is called publications co-ordinator because she does budgets that deal with publications. All of the jobs were defined in a certain way by the [personnel department] . . . and a "publications specialist" could do budgets, manage the office, edit, or any other number of things as far as the official job classification went. [The actual job description said] something about "create a library, do some work with publications, manage an office . . . a little bit of everything . . . I wasn't sure if I was going to be doing only budget and handle payroll or there would be a chance to do other things. . . . So, the description is not very concise for jobs in our office.

Joan's move to publications specialist meant a promotion to grade 20, the highest nonexempt job in the publications office. While the ambiguous nature of the job might have given some applicants second thoughts, its ambiguity proved an inducement for Joan.

Joan: That the job was not that strictly defined when I went to the job interview was one of the reasons that it appealed to me. I might end up doing only budgets but there might be a chance to do other things.

While nothing was guaranteed, there was at least the possibility of variety, and we have seen that Joan preferred juggling many jobs to one simple repetitive one. In this preference, she is not alone. Garson (1977) noted that workers doing routine work in a tuna packing plant, cosmetic company, lumber mill, auto plant, and other settings preferred doing different tasks to one repetitive one for any extended period of time.

What did Joan actually do when she first joined the publications office? As previously noted, she did many of the same things she did before: payroll, budget, filing, keeping track of people's hours and recording them, and ordering office supplies. As she put it: "It was quite awhile before anybody asked me if I would like to look at something and edit it or read it." But when they finally did, and she acquired some experience in reading and editing, she realized that she preferred editorial work to the repetitive and less-challenging jobs she had been doing. This led her to apply for the promotion that she was initially denied and ultimately awarded when she threatened to leave. Having achieved grade 45, exempt status, and the title of publications co-ordinator, she found herself doing many of the editorial and organizational tasks described in Chapter 2 and outlined in this chapter. In short, we have sketched what Joan previously did, what she is doing now, and the transition from the former to the latter. What has not yet received sufficient attention is the volume and diversity of the work she handled, and how (as in the quote by Orwell noted in Chapter 1) office work, like kitchen work, was difficult, not because of what each task required, but by virtue of the fact that one was under a tremendous time constraint to accomplish a wide range of jobs all to be done at the same time.

To get some idea of the volume of work, the university publications office handled about 4,000 separate printing jobs a year. These ranged from small jobs, such as office stationery, to big jobs, such as college bulletins and monographs. The total amount of paper handled is difficult to imagine. All of this material had to be read and edited, frequently more than once, as it passed back and forth between writers, editors, client servicepeople, designers, printers, and the clients themselves. In order to co-ordinate these efforts and people (all of whom had deadlines to meet) memos flowed freely. While it is impossible to know the number of memos generated annually (a number not included in the 4,000 jobs noted above), we can give some indication of the volume by considering the different types of memos routinely required to do business. There were "copy editing and change in document" memos, "production" memos, "information" memos, "contradiction resolution" memos, "information co-ordination" memos, and memos to and from "clients and client servicepeople." These and other memos were usually disposed of early in the morning during the time Joan donated to the university. These memos were dispatched not just to co-ordinate information on the status of various materials in the different stages of production, but also to co-ordinate people as well as things. This required the co-ordinator to arrange meetings and conferences for all relevant persons request-ing and/or providing publications services.

Things to be decided at these meetings (especially the formative ones) included when did the client need to have the product deliv-ered, how many copies, and how much money could they spend to purchase the needed services? All of these arrangements were made either through written memos or phone conversations, since none of the people requesting or providing these services were connected by E-mail. Written memos were especially prevalent for communicating outside the department. Other items needed in order to deliver publications services on time were dates for man-uscript submission, page proof completion, submission to printer, blueprints, and finally, a delivery date for the finished product. Notwithstanding the intricacies of this process and the many imponderables that had to be factored into this Byzantine produc-tion schedule, Joan estimated that 80 percent of all contracts were completed on time, 15 percent a few days late, and about 5 percent were as much as a month late. While some forms of printed mat-ter could be a few days late without producing dire consequences, some could not. Joan explained it this way:

> Award letters have to be sent out to prospective students to tell them what their financial aid is, and there's a date they have to be out by. Recruitment material and admissions pub-lications . . . have to be sent to all new students and all exist-ing students. So, there are deadlines. There are always ways to get around a deadline [for some publications]. If they don't have the publication that day they will hold up a mail-ing for a week. But that isn't always possible. When we had the reception for the opening [of a new building] they need[ed] those publications [on time]. There was no way of getting around it.

Because of all the services and people involved in the produc-tion schedule, Joan had to monitor and organize people and things every step of the way. This required not only good organi-zational skills, but good interactional skills. The publications office was not always one big happy family. We have seen how promotions were awarded so that one person's loss was another's gain. It goes without saying that this produced resentment among coworkers.

SOCIAL INTERACTION AND ORGANIZATIONAL DISCONTENT

Not everyone in the publications office was happy in their work. There were a number of causes for discontent. We have already seen that there was a competition for existing jobs. The grade 20 copyeditor's lament, Joan's disappointment at being denied a promotion, Joan and her former supervisor's disparate rates of advancement, and the replacement of the old director, are all examples of the potential for resentment generated by the scarcity of rungs on the upper reaches of the career ladder. Other causes also exist. One cause involved Joan's promotion.

Joan: [I worked in] the same office and with the same people [before and after her promotion]. It was an interesting transition because I went from the person who manages the office (in some people's eyes, I think I was considered an underling) to someone who is working at the same level and on the same kinds of projects as they were working on. It took them a while to make that transition [for them to be able to accept Joan as an equal].

Another example deals with the feeling of dislocation occasioned by the new director's restructuring of the office. This was another transition—one that the entire office had to get used to. During this period, morale was decidedly depressed. After workers got used to the restructured work setting, however, the reorganization plan gained acceptance and morale showed a marked improvement. The following excerpt refers to the time when the old director was leaving and the new one was coming on.

Joan: At that time they decided that they would reorganize where people sit. We were divided between two floors [the editors and writers and clerical staff]. What they did was they changed people around . . . the new boss thought if he got them together they could [work more efficiently]. So he decided to merge them with us, so they'd be closer to the editors and writers. . . . What this did was create a big hassle. First of all, people were very upset—not upset because we were getting a new boss, but [because] any time there's a change it's not good. Some people take kindly to change and others don't. . . . When the proposal to move people around came, it created a lot of human outcry. The people that went upstairs—some of the writers and editors [were] perceived of as the creative people in the office and the people who came downstairs—some people perceived of as pencil pushers. So, now we had a bunch of clerical people working with all the writers and editors.

The restructuring initially fostered apprehension and unhappiness for many, if not most, of the workers in the office. First, it moved people from familiar work settings and associations without their advice or consent. It was not just change that was the objection. Some of the discontent resulted from the intermingling of the "creative people" (the writers and editors) with the "pencil pushers" (the clerical help), who were understood in this setting to be the not-so-creative people.

In brief, the abrupt and forced reorganization of the office conflicted with the dictates of "consciousness of kind" (Giddings, 1896). Most of the office help were, and preferred to be, "among their own kind." The result was that workers were obliged during the transition period to get used to potential sources of conflict at many levels. Joan noted that

the people who came downstairs were also apprehensive about being downstairs because they had never worked with all of us before [the writers and editors] so they were tending to hold back and not be very friendly, because they weren't sure that we wanted to be there [with them] either. It has taken everyone a couple of months to realize that it's a good working relationship . . . so what is happening has really forced us to work together with client services, and people that we never would have worked with before. It has created much better social interaction. There's more chitchat at the coffee pot, or somebody will walk over and talk to somebody else, where for a couple of months, nobody did that. The client services people would visit with each other. The editors and writers would visit with each other. But there wouldn't be much interaction [between them].

Apart from creating a higher level of casual on-the-job forms of interaction, the restructuring also created, at least for some, friendships that resulted in off-the-job socializing.

I: Did you make any friends on the job . . . people you saw after [work] hours?
Joan: Yeah, I think that friendships did develop there [at the office] with administrators and also people in other academic offices—not necessarily with secretaries but [those at] a bit higher level.

Finally, restructuring of the office not only enhanced levels of communication between work groups, which increased levels of social interaction, but it increased productivity as well. Joan describes the situation prior to the new director's takeover:

It was a different work style with the old director. We always laughed and said that we worked in a communications office but we didn't know anything about what was going on. He [the old director] never shared information with anybody. We hardly ever had staff meetings. We never knew what was going on.

The new director's position on the need for open communication was different:

[With the new director] we have weekly staff meetings and monthly staff meetings. The weekly meetings have representatives from each section [editors, client services, design, and writers]. And then they go back and tell their groups what happened and then their concerns go to the next meeting and every four weeks it [the job of representing your section] rotates to someone else. So it's nice because there's much more open communication and those meetings have created a lot of social contacts, too, because people are in meetings together that would ordinarily not be sitting together and discussing anything.

All of the above led to greater productivity in the following way:

I think [that the open communications and higher levels of social interaction between all the office workers] helped us get along better. I think there are instances where you think you're not getting what you need from one of your co-workers and this sets up a really bad adversarial situation. Being more friendly socially with these people [co-workers] has actually made that adversarial confrontation thing happen less often. . . . And then the jobs go. They progress. They get printed. They get delivered [and] you can start on something else. [If you didn't get to know your co-workers] you really think that the whole job is being sabotaged [by them]. You know that person [the one you're in charge of] gets to think you're a real bitch and then the whole thing goes around— the job doesn't get delivered on time, you're working forever on it, there are mistakes, and you have to reprint it. So, I'm a firm believer in good communications between people that are working [together]—that's the key.

We have seen how and why the new director's reorganization plan led initially to a "human outcry" and lower morale but ultimately to enhanced morale and higher levels of interaction and productivity. More generally, the nature of work in a university publications office has been outlined as it was experienced by the workers in the course of conducting their everyday affairs.

4

Good Work and Bad Jobs: Ann, Principal Administrative Analyst

> Work may be a source of livelihood or the most significant part of one's inner life; it may be experienced as expiation or as exuberant expression of self, or as the development of man's universal nature. Neither love nor hatred of work is inherent in man or inherent in any given line of work, for work has no intrinsic meaning. (Mills, 1956:215)

A common aspect of work is the feeling that its routine features are boring and intrinsically unsatisfying. Much has been written on the consequences of capitalism's attempt to rationalize, systemize, and control production and labor (Mills, 1956; Braverman, 1974; Jacobs, 1971; and Garson, 1988). As a result, meaningful labor was reduced to a series of rationalized component parts that could be done by almost anyone. This expanded division of labor allowed for the interchangeability of workers on any kind of production line doing almost any sort of simple repetitive task. In addition, there was a high level of prediction and control. The advantage to this process was the rationalization of labor and the maximization of production and profits. The disadvantage was the alienation of labor, resulting from the expansion of the routinization and trivialization of work. The worker increasingly lost control over the ownership of the means of production and the end product of labor. Work that was once meaningful was reduced to a series of meaningless, repetitive tasks. The value of work in the pre- and postindustrial periods (and how it affected the workers' experience of work) also changed dramatically. According to many authorities, the Puritan values of sobriety, frugality, self-control, and a belief in hard work as a virtue have for the most part disappeared in the postindustrial period. Other sociologists and social historians think the opposite. They believe that many of the values formerly associated with the work ethic (see Weber, 1958) are still held by American workers.

Through the use of case study material, we will see in this chapter that the position of Mills as stated in the opening quote of this chapter is sound: "Neither love nor hatred of work is inherent in man or inherent in any given line of work, for work has no intrinsic meaning." This chapter will also show that the worker's assessment of the work he or she does is not a function of the work per se, but is primarily the product of a negotiated reality based on a series of on-the-job interactions with others sharing the same work setting. This contention will be documented with verbatim accounts of workers.

We have already seen in the preceding chapter how this was true for Joan. Case study material in this chapter will compare Joan's perception of office work, as a publications co-ordinator, with the assessment of Ann, a principal analyst in student affairs. We will see that these jobs have much in common. Both are with a university, entail a good deal of office work, were perceived of as providing good pay and benefits, are part of a bureaucratic structure and are subject to the constraints inherent in such structures (Jacobs, 1969), and entail many of the same kinds of tasks and skills—working at a word processor, writing memos, attending meetings, filing, and co-ordinating tasks and people. Further similarities include problems with superiors, acquiring job-relevant information from one's superiors or from written reports or policy statements, lack of formal training, and the extensive use of and the painful learning process associated with "on-the-job training." Of course, these two jobs are not the same in every regard. For example, they are at different universities, in different departments, in different geographic locales, and subject to different pay scales; one is union, one is not. Given the structural similarities and the routine, day-to-day requirements of the job, however, one could argue that the jobs of publications co-ordinator and principal analyst in student affairs have a great deal in common. Notwithstanding all the commonalities, we will see that the work was experienced differently by Joan and Ann, two middle-echelon university office workers. It was also experienced differently by Joan in the first twenty years of her career life than in the last seven.

For example, we have seen that Joan is currently happy with her job. She feels she is making good progress up the career ladder, believes her superior appreciates her efforts, recently gained a number of promotions and salary and benefit increases, and is not overly bothered by the constraints of bureaucracy. In contrast, we will see that Ann is not happy with her current job, feels she is overpaid, feels unappreciated by her superiors, is motivated to do a good job, and feels imprisoned by bureaucratic constraints.

While some or perhaps all of these diametrically opposed experiences could be attributed to differences in the basic personality of the two workers, it appears that nurture is a better explanation of these differences than nature. We will see from the case study that follows that Ann was subject to different sets of on-the-job circumstances than Joan, and that these explain her attitudes toward work better than arguments based on the intrinsic nature of work or any innate differences between the two. To see how, we will look at Ann's employment background.

CAREER PATH

While Joan's and Ann's current jobs have much in common, their career paths were different. For example, although they are approximately the same age, Ann acquired her Ph.D. in sociology from a major university in 1971, while Joan is still working toward her bachelor's degree. In the twenty years prior to her coming to the university, Joan had only three jobs. In the fifteen-year period prior to Ann's full-time employment with the university, she had approximately eighteen jobs and/or career changes. Both Joan and Ann have done a lot of office work in that time. Ann, however, held a variety of higher level jobs including counseling, teaching, consulting, and research. Until recently, Joan was restricted to lower-echelon office work. Most of Joan's employment was full time; most of Ann's was part time. Joan has been a working single parent longer than Ann, but Ann's financial situation has always been better. Both have been married, divorced, and have two children. In this chapter, we will see how the above circumstances, in conjunction with their formal education, the types of training they received, and the highest degrees earned (and when) helped account for Joan and Ann's different career paths and current attitudes toward work.

The following list outlines Ann's career path for the past twenty years, indicating as closely as possible the dates of each turning point. It will then be shown how Ann ended up as a principal administrative analyst and how, notwithstanding their different employment backgrounds, Joan's current job (publications coordinator) is very similar to Ann's.

1. Ann received her Ph.D. in sociology from a major West Coast university in 1971.

2. Instead of teaching, she "took a year off" so that she could recuperate from her dissertation and so that her husband could pursue his academic career.

3. During her year off she had a second child, earlier than she and her husband had planned, and the one-year break resulted in a series of events that spelled the beginning and end of Ann's academic career as a university professor.

4. During 1974–75, Ann attempted to enter the university academic job market with no success. "I started looking around for a part-time teaching position and discovered that in the interim [the two years she was at home caring for her children] the teaching profession seemed to have filled up."

5. During this time, Ann got a community college teaching credential, hoping to get a part-time position teaching at a community college. Unfortunately, she found that the part-time positions were no longer being filled, and full-time work was more than she could manage. "A full-time load seemed more than I could handle at that time."

6. She "started to look around for something else to do—
not necessarily as a money-making effort, but just to get
out of the house and keep my mind alive." At this point
she began working one day a week as a volunteer at
Planned Parenthood.

7. About 1978, her volunteer job became a half-time paid
position as a pregnancy and abortion counselor with
Planned Parenthood, which was, as Ann noted, "a fair
departure from classroom sociology."

8. About this time, Ann became certified as a childhood
educator. With her certification, she began to teach childhood education at Planned Parenthood.

9. Some time later, she taught childhood education at an
adult school for about five years and at a local hospital
for another three. All of these part-time positions paid
very little and provided few or no benefits.

10. After Planned Parenthood, she looked for and found a
state-funded position as a health planner with the job
title of health planning analyst. In this job, she did
research on at-risk newborns at a local hospital. This
soft-money job lasted about a year and a half.

11. Ann then moved to a half-time university-based funded
research job that lasted three years (approx. 1982–85).
Her title during this time was associate research specialist.

12. About halfway through this research position, she went
back to teaching birth classes for Planned Parenthood
because "I hadn't any luck in finding something else."

13. Concurrently, she started looking for consulting jobs
(approx. 1980) and found one with the county health
department, where she worked as a consultant one day
a week. Her title was health services consultant. That
grant lasted three years (1980–83), at which time she
began looking elsewhere.

14. In 1981, she taught a class (as an adjunct professor) at a
local college.

15. In 1983, she began working for the county on a three-fourths time basis as a data analyst. Then, in 1985, "the situation with the county became unbearable. The boss was a little wacko. Three of us left very quickly."

16. Upon leaving that job, she found another at the university in the summer of 1985 as a senior administrative analyst in the office of the vice president for health affairs. This was a full-time job ("a very full-time job") and the first one that Ann had held since she left teaching many years before.

17. At that point, Ann gave up teaching the birth classes for Planned Parenthood because "it was too much at once."

18. She held the senior administrative analyst position from the summer of 1985 to about January 1990, when she was promoted and shifted to another university program.

19. In January 1990, Ann moved from Health Affairs to Student Affairs where she currently works as a principal administrative analyst.

PUSH AND PULL FACTORS: MOTIVATIONS AND INCENTIVES FOR CAREER CHANGES

Ann underwent as many as eighteen career-employment changes in twenty years. What motivated these changes? This question requires a complicated and somewhat convoluted answer. In 1971, Ann and her husband earned their Ph.D.s. He went on to teach; she did not. Why not? First and foremost, she didn't have to. In 1971, Ann, her husband, and one small child could live on the entry-level academic salary that her husband earned. Second, she was relieved to be able to take a break, having spent the preceding year or two as a mother and a doctoral student. Third, she looked forward to being a mother and having the time to spend with her child, and finally, doing all the above would help her husband advance his academic career. While there is no way to weigh each of these items, all four figured prominently in keeping Ann out of the workplace during the period immediately following her graduation.

A couple of years later (1974–75), Ann (who now had a second child) tried to find a part-time academic teaching job with no success. Here again, there were a number of reasons. By this time the availability of university teaching jobs began to dwindle. It was the tail-end of the 1960s academic boom, and it was no longer a buyer's market. The permanent tenure-track jobs that were still available at the university level were full-time jobs, not part time. And within that category of possibilities, one could no longer pick and choose one's place of employment. To get a job, one had to be prepared to go to wherever the job presented itself. Even if she had wanted to work full time, she was not prepared to split her family to do so; consequently, she had essentially removed herself from the academic marketplace. These were some of the pull factors that kept Ann from becoming an academic.

Let's look now at some of the push factors motivating her to enter the academic job market in the first place. First there was her husband's salary. It was now a couple of years and a second child later, and his salary provided only a shrinking lifestyle. Financially speaking, they were downwardly mobile. Second, Ann liked teaching, thought she would be good at it, and looked forward to doing it. Third, she felt that the occupation of "homemaker" was not very challenging. She wanted something to "keep my mind alive." When she realized she could not find a part-time university teaching position in the same locale as her husband, she acquired a community college teaching credential with the hope of finding a part-time teaching job at the community college level. This, too, proved futile.

In order to do something, she sought and found a volunteer position with Planned Parenthood. About a year and a half later, this became a half-time paid position in a pregnancy and abortion clinic. After three years at Planned Parenthood, she felt the need to change jobs again. As Ann put it:

> Three years in the abortion clinic is as much as any human being ought to do. It's just like you start to lose perspective and you lose your ability to be a decent counselor, to be helpful to people. It's a very depressing and oppressive business. . . . It's a fast burnout job. I was there as a paid employee a little over a year, and that was it. I couldn't take it any more.

We can see how a job that Ann initially sought in order to "keep her mind alive" was, after three years, having the reverse effect. It was now more than she could bear, and the initial pull factor attracting her to the position ultimately worked to push her from it in ways that she could never have anticipated. There was, however, an advantage to the Planned Parenthood job. It provided what she does not have in her current position and now values most—complete autonomy and a good, or at least satisfactory, working relationship with her colleagues. On balance, however, the "depressing and oppressive" nature of the work outweighed the positive features, and Ann left. It should also be noted that the abortion counseling was not the sort of work that she hoped to get. As Ann put it, it was "a fair departure from classroom sociology."

In order to get back into teaching, Ann became a certified childhood educator. With her credentials in hand, she taught childhood education for Planned Parenthood, adult education classes for about five years, and at a local hospital for about three. These were all part-time jobs that provided low incomes and little or no benefits. Ann took them because they were the only part-time positions she could find and because they allowed her to do some form of teaching.

All in all, Ann was enthusiastic about her employment with the county as a health planning analyst and later as a consultant. She expressed the advantages of this work as follows:

> The work I did at the county was wonderful. I couldn't believe they were paying me to do that [because she enjoyed it so much, and] because it was what I'd been doing at that time. I had been doing research on infant and natal mortality and morbidity, writing reports, and reviewing literature. It was just terrific.

The problem with these jobs was not the work but the boss:

> The problem was, the boss wouldn't let anything out of his office. He was completely paranoid. Everybody boycotted

our unit because we weren't providing the services we were supposed to. And he promoted two or three of his favorite people into advisory positions over the rest of us, and we knew they were a lot dumber than we were. So, three of us left [in protest]. So, again, the work atmosphere was awful, but the work was great.

Here again, we see the net effects of push and pull. The pull factors were strong. Ann enjoyed the work and the company of a number of her fellow workers. Unfortunately, the push factors were stronger, and she and two of her colleagues, who could not tolerate the boss for a variety of reasons, decided to leave.

Without going through every one of Ann's eighteen career moves in nineteen years, we can see that understanding her career is a complicated issue in terms of push-pull factors. It requires a detailed description of her jobs, as well as an understanding of her acceptance and rejection of different kinds of work settings and relationships. It is significant to note that while Ann quit a number of jobs, she was never fired. She left only because of her personal distaste for her immediate superiors, a lack of autonomy, her superiors' lack of appreciation for her work, and/or their inability to recognize and utilize her full potential. Rarely did Ann quit a job because of poor pay and benefits. While a generous salary and benefits might serve, as they currently do, to keep her in a job she might otherwise leave, poor pay and benefits did not motivate her to change jobs. More often than not, Ann's reasons for leaving a job were not motivated exclusively or even primarily by rational self-interest, and this was true of Joan as well.

Without the detailed information that these case studies provide, it would be impossible to understand the career paths of these two women. Economic models of worker behaviors based exclusively on self-interest offer little if any promise in such an undertaking. While this model is prevalent, not all economists subscribe to it. Frank (1988) argues that people do not always act in their self-interest, and paradoxically, it would not be in their self-interest if they did. This was true in Joan's case. We will see that it may be true for Ann as well.

DIMENSIONS OF CAREER DEVELOPMENT

Hard Work

Ann, like Joan, was a hard worker. Some indication of her industry was that she felt she was paid too much, not too little. Given what she felt were the arbitrary constraints of bureaucracy and her immediate superiors, and the way in which both worked to trivialize her work, Ann felt that someone with a much lower level of expertise could do her job and that the university was wasting its money by not utilizing her full potential. Ann tells us, "It's ridiculous. I'm paid $47,300 a year to do what any competent secretary could do. Of course, there aren't many of those around anymore." Ann knew this from firsthand experience. She and the assistant director shared a series of secretaries that both felt were incompetent and who stayed for only a very short time. This was true of the university setting that Joan worked in as well.

The irony was that Ann felt she could truly earn her salary and feel better about herself if only her boss would let her. As she saw it, she had a number of good ideas for improving efficiency at the routine office level and in terms of the more serious work she did that involved evaluating proposed legislative bills and their effects on the university and student affairs. A number of factors, however, worked against her ability to achieve this sense of fulfillment.

First, Ann felt that she could not work up to her potential because of an information gap. When she tried to find out what she should or could do about work-related problems, she found it impossible to obtain relevant information, either from official published policy statements or by asking her immediate superior. The former (if they existed) were nowhere to be found, while the latter usually offered contradictory suggestions or none at all. This coupled with her boss's aversion to formal training and the almost total reliance on learning through doing led Ann to experience chronic frustration. Her perception of the job was that she spent a great deal of time looking for things, or dealing with problems that should have taken no time at all. Ann put it this way:

> My current job is very frustrating as it seems very difficult to get hold of any information. I don't know how to find out

what I need to know. It's a new experience for me. I've always been pretty good in finding out what I need to know, but I'm damned if I know where to go [now]. If I want to find something in the files I have to open every single one of the file drawers.

I: Because they're not systematically filed?

Ann: No [they're not]. And I have raised this issue with the boss several times, and she's not willing to do anything about it. So, it's time consuming and tedious and very inefficient. And this is the only place I've ever worked where I can't even find a pencil. *I've had to bring my own pencils* [emphasis added]. Even the county [job] had pencils. . . . So, I'm in the process of setting up my own working files. When I find something that has information [I need], I make a copy and I put it somewhere I know I can find it for future reference.

In addition to an information gap and its effects on office efficiency and morale, Ann felt that the assistant director did not appreciate the work she did and, worse still, unjustly punished her. These disciplinary actions took a number of different forms. One revolved around the contradiction between the official university position that workers at Ann's level were "professionals" and her superiors' treatment of her as a "time-clock puncher."

There's a very funny conflict between treating us as professionals and treating us as people who punch a time clock. . . . It's rather schizophrenic. On the one hand you're supposed to be available to work late, or if your conference starts on Sunday, you're supposed to be willing to pick up at noon on Sunday and go there. But on the other hand, if you come in late you'd better have a damn good reason. . . . I came in late one morning, and I was told I had to take vacation time to cover the time I was late. . . . I had been taking work home. I had worked through lunch. I kept a fair balance in my head about how much time [I spent working]. I stayed half an hour yesterday and did an hour's work at home. [Under the circumstances], it doesn't seem criminal to me to come in a half hour late. But I was instructed that I needed to take [that

half hour off my vacation time] like I'm being punished. . . .
The director [her boss] comes in late whenever she likes.

What Ann described is an informal one-way flex time
arrangement that favors the university. Under this format,
Ann's time is to be flexible so that she is on tap whenever the
university needs her. A commitment to this policy is also seen as
part of her "professional" status. Flex time, however, doesn't
apply when she requires time to deal with her off-the-job personal problems. In these cases, she is treated as a nonprofes-
sional "time-clock puncher." Here, we see the discrepancy
between the job description (official company policy) and the
actual dictates of the job. As noted earlier, the unanticipated discrepancy between the two, especially when it consistently
favors the organization, leads to low morale, disenchantment,
or alienation. This was certainly true in Ann's case. Conversely,
the expectation of flex time coupled with the idea of professionalism can lead to higher morale and productivity when they are
equitably applied, as was true in Joan's case. Ann's case graphically illustrates the effects of one's superiors arbitrarily abridg-
ing formal sets of policy expectations.

The director and assistant director of Ann's unit exercised a
great deal of discretionary power in deciding whether or not to
honor the formal rights, privileges, and expectations that accom-
pany the status of "professional." This occurred notwithstanding
formal organizational structures intended to limit these discretionary powers. Ann tells us:

You need to conform to the rules of bureaucracy. They (her
bosses) have very little time and patience for you if you
don't. It is increasingly clear that there are no benefits in not
conforming. It also seems to me to be fairly unjust. Clearly
people don't get rewarded on the basis of the quality of their
work in spite of all the lip service through their hiring [pro-
cedures]. You [those doing the hiring] can manage to find
ways around it [the rules of bureaucracy]—people manage
to. If they want to appoint someone, they do. So you see people who appear not to be doing a particularly good job, or
people who don't seem to be doing any better than oneself,

moving up the ladder. So the bureaucracy part of it is getting very hard to take.

The operation of real versus a "symbolic bureaucracy" has been noted elsewhere (Jacobs, 1969).

We have seen how Joan's boss, because he was happy with her performance, was scrupulous in honoring these privileges, while Ann's boss, who was unhappy, chose not to. To add insult to injury, she disciplined Ann whenever possible. Regarding this exercise of power, one of two explanations is possible: Ann's boss chose not to honor Ann's professional status because Ann was in fact incompetent, or Ann's boss, because of her own incompetence, could not appreciate Ann's contribution.

Management's assessment of worker performance usually turns on two rational organizational considerations: level of productivity and the quality of the product produced. In office settings, the former is frequently easier to measure than the latter. For example, one could count (with the aid of computers) how many letters, words, or keyboard strokes one averaged over an eight-hour day and have a reasonable measure of productivity (Garson, 1988). The *quality* of office work, however, cannot be measured with a micrometer, as it might be in a machine shop. In office work, we are dealing with a much more subjective assessment of work when it comes to quality control. Inasmuch as the product of office work is usually words and paper and not nuts and bolts, the assessment often has to be based on some evaluation of the presentation of words, as well as what the words convey—form as well as content. This leads ultimately to such a question as, "Was Ann as good a writer as her boss?" This, in fact, became a key factor in Ann's boss's evaluation of her performance.

In principle, we can see that Ann's superior had to assess two major components of her work. First, was she doing a good job of evaluating the potential effects of pending legislation on the university and, second, could she formulate these assessments in some acceptable writing style? In any rational consideration of things, one might expect greater emphasis to be placed on the content than the form. It would seem more important to decide if Ann was accurate in her assessment of the effects of legislative bills on university student affairs than to worry about the written expression of these assessments as they appeared in memos, letters, or reports. Did Ann and her boss usually agree with Ann's analysis of pending bills? The answer is "yes." Her boss seemed satisfied that Ann was capable of reading, interpreting, and analyzing the contents of legislative bills and assessing their effects on the university. She was, however, often unhappy with the written form of these evaluations. The general problem was as follows. The assistant director believed that there was a right way to write reports (her way), and a wrong way (Ann's), and that it was her duty to scrupulously enforce the right way. Ann attributed this rigidity to a boss who was too bureaucratically constrained for the unit's, the university's, and/or Ann's good. From her perspective, the boss's commitment to one way of doing and expressing everything led to gross inefficiencies and low levels of productivity and morale. The following are some examples:

> I've been very argumentative, both with the boss, . . . and when she was on vacation, the assistant boss, about their correcting my syntax a lot. Whatever I write comes back to me three or four times with changes in syntax of the kind that I think are not only unnecessary but absurd. You know there are things that are a [matter of] preference and I feel that if people are so adamant about the style, then they need to be writing their own letters [Ann ghost-writes most of the assistant director's and director's letters for them]. If you are going to hire staff to write for you, you have to be able to be a little bit flexible and willing to accept something that is maybe not the same kind of phrasing you would use. But the focus in my unit is on everything being perfect [in form]. Well, half of what goes out of there is not perfect and almost everything that goes out of there, is up to three weeks late because so much time is spent on [petty] details [only 5 percent of all work in Joan's office left weeks late]. So, I'm spending huge amounts of time rewriting stuff on the order of: "I'm responding to you on behalf of the president [of the university]," and it will come back reading: "On behalf of the president, I am responding."
> I: Well, let's put it another way. If you were reading a report she wrote, do you think it would look any better than the one you wrote?

Ann: I don't think so. It's much more formal language than I would use. In general, bureaucratic language is more elaborate than my personal style. I tend to write in a fairly elliptical style and so that always comes back expanded. And so [trying to please] I've been expanding. And it's coming back contracted.

Temperament

In keeping with one classical model for dealing with adversity, Ann could have dealt with her superiors in one of two ways: flight or fight. First, as her friends and colleagues repeatedly recommended, she could have made whatever corrections her boss suggested without comment. This strategy recommends compliance coupled with indifference. Humoring her boss would reduce the level of conflict, ensure regular promotions, provide job security, and reduce Ann's blood pressure. In short, it was recommended in this form of adaptation that one "make the best of a bad situation," "not make waves," take a generous salary, and "laugh all the way to the bank." While many in like circumstances could and would pursue this course of rational self-interest, Ann could not. What's more, we have seen how, for different reasons, Joan was also unable to pursue self-interest in an unbridled way.

The second strategy in the flight or fight model would be to rebel and try to demonstrate the absurdity of some of the standard bureaucratic practices that had become a part of Ann's work setting. This is the tack she took, not only in self-defense, but for self-preservation. More conscientious and idealistic than most, she never really learned how to live a lie for any prolonged period of time. Recognizing early the absurdity of many of the work practices she encountered in the office, she found it difficult to live by them and to continue working in what she perceived to be a theater of the absurd. We have already seen how and why societal members generally are unable to live in a random universe and are always creating for themselves structure and order out of what is, according to some social theorists, an inherently random and absurd life and social world. In this model, those who can adapt most readily to the inherent absurdity of the social world are those who have managed by whatever means to take life and work for granted, that is, to accept most of what they encounter in life in some unquestioning way. The others, those who recognize and cannot accept the absurdity, are obliged to live a problematic existence. The former (the "insiders") are threatened by the latter (the "outsiders") and often label them as troublemakers (Becker, 1973). This was the scenario in which Ann lived. When she tried to bring petty and arbitrary copyediting changes to the attention of her bosses and explain why they were not only unfair and absurd, but led to gross office inefficiencies and low morale, she was rebuked. This resulted in increased levels of frustration, which led ultimately to a state of emotional upset. Ann tells us: "I got upset and I yelled and screamed and carried on. And since then, they [her superiors] have clearly decided that I'm not trustworthy and they must tighten the reins and make sure that I [conform]. . . . I have been defined as a difficult employee. I'm a discipline problem." From this perspective, we can now see why her bosses' discretionary powers were used not for, but against, her.

In comparing the different ways in which Joan and Ann dealt with potential conflict on the job, we see that they, more often than not, invoked different modes of adaptation. Joan was more likely to use flight (or system accommodation strategies) and Ann used fight (or system reform strategies). Since the latter is inherently more confrontational, Ann got into trouble more often than Joan. Again, one can attribute these different forms of dealing with adversity to differences in personality. A case can be made for this position. However, a stronger case can be made for interactional factors.

First, in terms of their current employment situations, Joan's boss was fair and reasonable; appreciative of her work; rewarded her with raises, promotions, and flex time; gave her a wide range of autonomy in terms of work practices to do as she thought best; and finally, kept the lines of communication open at all levels. As a result, Joan was a contented worker who was happy not only with the work that she did but with her boss and most of her co-workers. If all of these conditions were operating in Ann's office, the result would have been different. Unfortunately, they were not. Ann's boss was unreasonable, arbitrary, and unhappy with her work; did not reward and sometimes punished her for being conscientious; did not keep lines of communication open; provided little autonomy for what Ann understood to be a professional-level position providing a great deal of autonomy; and allowed for flex time only sometimes and then only after the demeaning ceremony of having Ann make a formal request for it in advance.

In short, if Joan got more than she hoped for when she applied for the job as publications co-ordinator (remember the job description was very ambiguous), then Ann got much less than she hoped for when she accepted the job of principal administrative analyst in student affairs. These outcomes are particularly ironic when we remember that Joan could have only hoped for the best, while Ann had every reason to expect the best. Ann's job description was unambiguous, as were the understandings she had as the result of her forthright discussion with the director. Both the job description and the director had given her every assurance that this was a well-paid, responsible, professional position that included a large measure of autonomy, flex time, interesting and challenging work, and open lines of communication—most of which she later found did not exist. Had she known this in advance, she would not have accepted the position in the first place, the generous salary notwithstanding. In fact, because of her dissatisfaction with her previous position, she went out of her way to clarify all these points with the director during her interview so as to avoid any future misunderstandings. None of this helped. While Ann was very impressed with the director during the interview, it turned out to be a case of misplaced optimism and a nasty instance of faulty first impressions (Schwartz and Jacobs, 1979). The agreement between the assurances she got during her interview (as well as those provided in writing in the job description) and what she actually encountered on the job approached zero.

When viewed from this frame of reference, the different levels of job satisfaction held by Joan and Ann are better understood as stemming from the different experiences they encountered in the workplace rather than as resulting from personality differences. After all, in terms of most other employment-relevant considerations, Joan and Ann had much in common. They were both hard workers; conscientious beyond the call of duty; competent beyond what any employer had reason to expect (neither had ever been fired from a job, both had been granted numerous promotions, and Ann had better academic credentials than either of her bosses); and both were friendly, personable, and forthright.

If on-the-job circumstances are important for understanding the work career and level of job satisfaction of these two women, off-the-job circumstances are no less important. We have already noted two key points in this regard. The first is that Ann has been more financially secure than Joan, and second, that Ann has a Ph.D., while Joan is still working to complete her bachelor's degree. These two facts had a profound influence on how they approached a prospective job, which jobs they approached, and their attitude toward work when on the job. To begin with, someone who is financially secure has more time and is under less pressure to accept the first job that comes along. Financial security allows an individual to pick and choose jobs and provides at least the potential for acquiring a job that offers a challenge, autonomy, job satisfaction, financial rewards, and the promise of advancement. What's more, those who have this luxury enjoy not only its initial benefits, but its potential long-term benefits, as well. High-status jobs tend to generate other high-status jobs. Low-status entry jobs tend to generate dead ends.

Coupling Ann's preferred financial standing with her higher academic and class status, we can see why Joan was under a greater social and economic obligation to "get along" on the job than Ann. It also helps to explain why Joan held only three low-level office jobs over a twenty-year period and why she was reluctant to abandon them even when she would have liked to. It allows us to see, as well, how Ann was able to quit a series of high-status jobs during that time and sample many others without undue concern for the consequences. Finally, it helps us to understand why Joan was likely to adopt a compromising, as opposed to challenging, stance toward her employer. After all, someone with a Ph.D. and financial security is in a much better position to be independent about what they expect of a job (and their colleagues) than someone without a college degree and only marginal financial resources. The career paths of these two middle-echelon university office workers and their attitudes toward work during their careers bear this out.

A comparative outline of Joan's and Ann's employment careers has been provided to show how interactional and environmental factors on and off the job can be used to explain temperament, job satisfaction, and career paths without invoking personality theory. We have seen how two women working in different universities; in different work settings; at different ends of the country; and holding different social, economic, and academic statuses, as well as different career paths, ended up in office jobs that were similar. This, it is contended, need not be as surprising as it first seems for two reasons. First, we have seen how Ann seemed to have every opportunity to achieve the university academic position she wanted but was prevented from doing so by a series of real-life circumstances, some within and some beyond her control. She ended up instead in an unfulfilling low-level administrative position that she felt "any competent secretary could do." However, her current low level of morale and job satisfaction did not result from feelings of "relative deprivation" (Merton, 1957). The problem was not that Ann felt she might have been a college professor but ended up a high-paid secretary. Actually, she liked her work. The problem was the feeling she had that she was not allowed to fulfill her potential while on the job and that her bosses and their bureaucratic mentality were to blame for this state of affairs. In brief, the problem with the job was not the work itself. This she viewed as neither beneath her nor potentially uninteresting. Rather, it was the way in which her superiors defined the job that had trivialized it and made office work not only inefficient but absurd.

A critical aspect of work that has not been discussed yet is the effect of increasing age in an ageist and sexist society. While it is true older men have a harder time finding jobs than equally qualified younger men, both younger and older women suffer from relative deprivation at all stages of the life course regarding most employment opportunities and the prospect of advancement. As a result, Joan found it harder to move up through the ranks of low-level secretarial positions, and Ann found it more difficult to become a college professor than her husband. Ageism and sexism, however, cannot explain the work careers of these two women per se. Other women in similar or worse situations twenty years ago ended up tenured full professors at colleges and universities. I know a number of them. Conversely, a number of the most promising males who graduated from University of California,

Los Angeles, with a Ph.D. in sociology on or about the time that I did (1967) are no longer sociologists or college professors. These include men whose first academic appointments were at Harvard and Yale. What's more, the prestige rankings of the jobs many of these graduates currently hold are lower, not higher, than college professor, for example, social worker, computer analyst, auto mechanic, and pornographic bookstore owner.

Recognizing the constraining effects of ageism and sexism, we can understand why Ann, who got a Ph.D. in 1971 but only acquired her first full-time academic job in 1985, might now hold the job of principal administrative analyst and not college professor. I say "might," because as we have seen, she might also have become a college professor. The fact is, no single or set of SES (socio-economic status) variables or demographic interpretations can explain the career paths of these two particular women. Nor can ageism and sexism per se satisfactorily explain why Joan, who spent twenty years in office work "going nowhere," suddenly got somewhere in seven years. An attempt to answer questions of this sort requires the kind of detailed data and analysis provided above.

Skills

What skills did Ann have that allowed her to do the work of a principal administrative analyst? It turns out that Ann and Joan needed to acquire many of the same skills. For example, Ann needed to know how to type, use a word processor, ghost-write letters and reports, search for and find buried information, photocopy and file documents, and answer the phone and talk to others in a businesslike way. Most of these skills Ann learned as a graduate student and found that they were easily transferable to her new setting years later. Some she learned recently, such as becoming a "proficient" word processor.

> You don't have to know how to type really good. I don't type but I can work a word processor. I never learned to type. . . . I type one finger. I'm very fast, but very inaccurate. You don't have to know how to spell anymore because the machine will do it for you. *I never learned to type [correctly]*

because I thought I never wanted to become a secretary. [emphasis added]

Other skills, such as reading legal and other formal documents, she learned while doing graduate research, although she picked up the special vocabulary associated with much of her day-to-day work as she went along. There was no formal training in this regard, nor did her employers see any reason to initiate any. We will see that Ann viewed this as one of the many oversights in office procedures that needed reform.

She also learned as part of her graduate training in sociology to do quantitative forms of statistical analysis. This skill she put to good use in her various health service jobs. Over the years, it also provided her with a number of job opportunities in the area of social science research. It should be noted, however, that the manipulation and interpretation of statistical data play only a very small role in her current job. What she actually does now, and the estimated time she spends doing it, will be considered next.

THE WORK OF A PRINCIPAL ADMINISTRATIVE ANALYST

Ann's involvement with student affairs has nothing to do with curriculum or the academic side of student life. Rather, she is involved with support services for students, such as child care, student loans and fees, health care, housing, and so on. In dividing her chores into categories, Ann gave the following account:

I: You have to draft letters, reports, and memos. How much time do you think you spend doing that?
Ann: Probably about 50 percent of my time. Most of this time is in front of the computer, partly because of this copyediting *mishugas* [Jewish word meaning "craziness"].

She is referring here to the director's and assistant director's practice of copyediting her written text. This entailed a number of corrected versions of the same text, since all final copies leaving the office had to be letter and form perfect. It was Ann's belief that the application of these procedures has led to gross inefficiencies and half of all the work going out three weeks late.

In addition to the 50 percent of her time spent generating "paper," Ann estimated that 20 percent is spent on the phone and another 10 percent on "housekeeping"—the time spent finding a pencil, sharpening it, walking to and from the photocopy machine, making copies, finding things in the cupboards—and another 10 percent finding randomly filed items in the file cabinets. The remaining 10 percent of her time is spent in meetings. The actual research, that is, reading and evaluating legislative bills to assess their potential impact on the university and student affairs, is included in the 50 percent of the time spent at her word processor and the 20 percent on the phone. Ann enjoys reading and evaluating bills and writing memos, letters, and reports. What she does not enjoy is having her immediate superiors critically assess every word. This left her feeling increasingly frustrated, not only because of the absurdity of these unnecessary and unwanted picayune efforts, but because of the increasing loss of control she felt over her own work.

> *I*: In terms of what you told me about the categories of work and their distribution, what would you like to be doing more of, or less of, that would increase your job satisfaction?
> *Ann*: I'm not sure I can answer that question because my dissatisfaction does not come necessarily from the nature of work. It comes from the lack of control of the work. So, 50 percent of my time doing research would be fine. I like writing. It's the fact that I have to conform to someone else's standards in everything I do that bothers me.

Another major area of concern for Ann, and others who work in her unit, was the time spent learning the hundreds of little things necessary to make the job doable. The extraordinary time and effort expended on getting relevant information because of the lack of formal training, coupled with the poor lines of communication, led not only to gross inefficiency, but to escalating frustration and deflated morale. An example of this is Ann's description of the frustration she and others felt at having to osmose special job-related vocabularies and policies.

One of the things you need to learn [because they don't tell you about it] is the structure of the university. And you have to learn that fast because you have to get your "cc's" in order.

By this she meant that if the secretary, analyst, assistant director, or director of the unit did not know how the university's hierarchy was structured, they would not know who was entitled to receive copies of their work or how to list those persons receiving copies in order of their descending rank.

My colleagues are very bad at doping out what people [who work in the office] don't know. And they speak in jargon. This makes it much more difficult to become a part of the team [especially when] they assume everyone already understands what they are saying. [For example], they say, "Well, he's the 504 of the campus." The what? I don't know what that is. Or, "He's the title IX officer." I don't know what that is! And they don't tell you. . . . They didn't tell me that I needed to know that there are universitywide policies on student organizations and conduct, which are written down. They constantly referred to these as "A & B." I was there for a month or more before I knew what the hell they were talking about and discovered that ["A & B"] was an important resource. . . . And, in fact, I noticed that they did very, very little training. There's been a lot of turnover. They didn't train me or any of the new secretaries that have [recently] come on. And I could see that even the secretary who was there when I arrived, who had been there awhile, didn't know anything.

In addition, there were innumerable other things that everyone working in the office, from the secretary to the director, needed to know and were obliged to learn about in one way or another. The following are some examples.

Ann: They got all the letterheads in a particular way. [First] you put the file name [on it] and then you put the initials of all the people who have to sign off on it. So, for example, if it's going to the president, you have the initials of the president, the assistant vice president, the director, the assistant director, your own, and the secretary's in a string, and then the date. Well, for reasons unknown to me, my colleague [the assistant director and Ann's immediate superior] will not put the string of initials at the top. She feels this is a secretarial function. I feel it helps me keep it straight. There's a lot of stuff like that. [Another example is] information is passed about in colored folders. If it's blue, it's for information. If it's red, then it's urgent action. If it's yellow, it's review, and if it's orange something else. And when it goes from our office to the AVP [assistant vice president's office], it all has to be transferred to a different colored folder. And then there are little slips that are used for tracking, and there's a logging system—when it came in, when it went out. So when we get a complaint, "What happened to so-and-so," we sometimes have to co-ordinate with other people [which means] we have to break into this chain somewhere, to send a copy out for them to review. There's a tremendous amount of this housekeeping stuff.

As we can see, there is endless minutiae that people doing office work have to learn and deal with in order for the work to get done. Much of this minutiae is binding across status positions— from director to secretary—personnel at all levels need to learn their file colored codes and how to get their "cc's" straight. In all of these and dozens of other ways, we can see how the trivia of office work cuts across status rankings, academic programs or departments, and university settings. Because of this, the work that Joan and Ann did, while different in some regards, was very similar in others. Ann and Joan could have switched jobs and, after a brief period of adjustment, probably have functioned as well in one as the other. This is true notwithstanding the fact that Ann's job title was different from Joan's, or that her salary was more than twice Joan's, or that they worked in different universities and in different programs.

In spite of these differences, each of these middle-echelon university office workers found their work intrinsically interesting and potentially satisfying. If there was a problem, it was not with the work, but rather with their bosses and/or co-workers. Garson

(1977) found the same thing. In her study, she was surprised to find that workers in a variety of settings doing boring, routine, repetitive jobs were for the most part satisfied with their work. Whether workers experienced high job satisfaction and high morale, or low job satisfaction and low morale seemed to depend less on the work itself (or even the salary and benefits) than on the satisfying interactions with bosses and co-workers and the feeling of some control over the work. These aspects of work offer greater potential for understanding work and workers and such work-related issues as job satisfaction, morale, commitment to the organization, term of employment and/or absenteeism than the idea of rational self-interest implied or stated in most economic theories. Ann expressed a similar sentiment when she said:

> They pay me a lot of money for what I do which is something of a rip-off. I don't feel so good about that, but hell, I'll take the money [she can't afford not to at this stage of her life given her current responsibilities]. It [the job] has great benefits, [and] good working conditions. *But, it's hard to go to work everyday in a place you feel people are going out of their way to put you down, and control you, and where you feel like, you know, you do have some skills and talents, something to offer, and nobody's bothering to use it* [emphasis added].

In keeping with Ann's feelings, others have noted the negative effects of abusive management styles (Hudson, 1991), worker intolerance for incompetent management (Crawford, 1989), or the worker's need for autonomous activity (Becker et al., 1961; Hudson, 1991). Hudson put it nicely when he said: "The analysis of worker's practical autonomy, its varieties, and its antecedents and consequences is a vast, little explored, and terribly important area in the sociology of work." We have seen how this applies to Joan's and Ann's cases and why "the differential ability of workers to engage in autonomous, self-defining activity at the work place is an important key to understanding their changing relative fortunes" (Hudson, 1991). This is true not only with regard to the need for autonomous activity, but for the other work-related issues as well.

5

God Bless the Children: Toni, Educator and Child Care Administrator

The origin of this distressful thing was this. . . . John Wilson Mackenzie, of Rotterdam, Chemung County, New Jersey, deceased, contracted with the General Government, on or about the 10th day of October, 1861, to furnish General Sherman the sum total of thirty barrels of beef. (Twain, 1958:40)

Mackenzie traveled worldwide in an unsuccessful attempt to deliver this beef to General Sherman. In the end he was killed. After the attempts of a long succession of relatives to collect from the federal government, the bill came to Mark Twain as an inheritance by way of a distant uncle.

I took this beef contract, and the bill for mileage and transportation, to the President of the United States . . . the Postmaster-General . . . Agriculture Department . . . Speaker of the House of Representatives . . . Commissioner of the Patent Office . . . and finally, the Treasury Department. . . .

He sent me to the Second Auditor. The Second Auditor sent me to the Third, and the Third sent me to the First Comptroller of the Corn-Beef Division. This began to look business. He examined his books and all contracts. I went to

the Second Comptroller of the Corn-Beef Division. He exam-
ined his books and his loose papers, but with no success. I
was encouraged. During that week I got as far as the Sixth
Comptroller in that division; the next week I got through the
Claims Department; the third week I began and completed
the Mislaid Contracts Department, and got a foothold in the
Dead Reckoning Department. I finished that in three days.
There was only one place left for it now. I laid siege to the
Commissioner of Odds and Ends. (Twain, 1958:41, 43)

And so Mark Twain's account goes on to relate his (and his prede-
cessors) valiant, but unsuccessful, attempt to collect the bill for
thirty barrels of beef, plus transportation, from the federal government, better understood here as the federal bureaucracy.

The effects of bureaucratic structures on workers cannot be
overemphasized. As we have seen and will see, all the professional women in this book worked in bureaucratic settings. Joan
worked for a private bureaucracy; Ann worked for a state bureaucracy. Toni (in this chapter) worked for the federal bureaucracy,
and Fran and Freda (in the chapters that follow) for county
bureaucracies. None of these women described their involvement
with bureaucracy in positive terms. Rather, it was always seen as
something that one had to contend with, overcome, subvert, get
around, or accommodate, in order to get any work done. This is
odd, given Weber's formulation of bureaucracy as the best way to
organize large-scale work programs rationally (Gerth and Mills,
1946:196–224). If true, why do these professional women see it as
an obstacle rather than an asset for getting work done? The need
to subvert the workings of ideal ("symbolic") bureaucracies has
been dealt with elsewhere (Jacobs, 1969).

It should also be noted that the women in this study found that
the greater the scope and effects of the bureaucracy, the more dis-
agreeable the job. For example, Joan was better able to contend
with private bureaucracy (moderated by academic collegiality)
than Ann, Toni, Fran, or Freda who had to deal with the ubiquitous effects of state, federal, or county bureaucracies.

In this chapter, we will see that working in a bureaucratic setting means spending most of one's time and energy not in pursuing the avowed goals of the agency, but in subverting the

constraints of bureaucracy that make the accomplishment of those goals almost impossible.

CAREER PATH

Toni graduated from a major university with a master's degree in anthropology in 1963. Unable to find a job, she returned to college for a teaching credential. "Get a teaching credential," her parents told her. "You can always get a job no matter what." In late 1963 she had progressed as far as her student teaching when she decided "this was not for me." Toni found that she had a hard time handling a classroom of children. "It was much more an interpersonal relations thing than I thought." After about six months of working toward her teaching credential, she dropped out (in the spring semester of 1964).

Toni then started working full time at what had been a part-time job during her college career, doing laboratory work in a hospital. At this juncture she believed she was about to begin a third career as a histology technician.

> I thought I was going to get all kinds of training and become a hot-shot researcher. But it turned out to be nothing but very routine, mundane, tedious work where I watched the clock all day long. So I finally decided that if I was going to be unhappy in my job, I might as well be unhappy in something where I was going to get paid more for, so I went back to student teaching.

This time, however, her student teaching was in a "totally different environment, a totally different teacher, and totally different group of children. And I really loved it." At this point in her career, Toni became interested in the politics of educational reform. This new-found interest was to a large extent the product of time and place. It was 1964, Berkeley, California. "Things were really interesting," she said. "The curriculum development that was going on—everything was so innovative and there was a lot of staff interaction."

When she completed her degree in education and got her teaching credential, she was offered three jobs. She accepted a position teaching fifth and sixth grades with one of the smaller schools in a neighboring town because she liked the interviewers and the interview questions. It was an exciting time for Toni, and she described it this way: "The staff was very consolidated and we spent a lot of time together, and we talked about the children, we talked about problems, and I really felt at home with the children, the parents, and the staff."

Shortly after beginning this job (about 1965), another turning point occurred. She took a class in "nonauthoritarian teaching in the classroom" conducted by Paul Goodman and a number of other major figures in American liberal education. It changed her life.

> I just got very interested, not just in teaching but [in] the whole learning aspect and how education fits into the social system, where change comes from, and what schools are all about. And I decided that I needed to know more about how it started and what younger children were like.

In order to explore these questions, Toni managed to get a job as a kindergarten teacher in her school after convincing the principal that he should give her the job if she took a summer class at the state college on how to teach kindergarten. She had already seen kindergarten taught in her school and was unimpressed with what she saw: "I went to visit the classroom and I didn't like what I saw at all. Even though I knew very little about teaching kindergarten, I knew it wasn't good teaching."

Once again, her self-actuated approach to learning paid off. The class she took was "another really uplifting experience in teaching because that was the [state college] laboratory school with a wonderful master teacher and a wonderful program. And it was another eye-opening experience for me on what a classroom could really be like."

In the fall of 1968, after teaching fifth and sixth grades for three years, Toni began to teach kindergarten.

> I started teaching in the kindergarten room and then something [happened] that is very significant in my teaching career. The enrollment dropped, so I only had a class in the

morning. So, in the afternoon I would go to another elementary school and team teach with another kindergarten
teacher. And, it was at that point it all kind of came together
for me, what I wanted to do with kids and how to do it.

She continued in that situation for about a year. At that point,
she discovered a new program at the state college dealing with
early childhood education. Toni also found out that schools who
participated in this program were eligible to receive funding. She
arranged an appointment with the assistant superintendent of
schools and told him about the program and the funding it could
bring the school district. As a result, her school became one of the
first in the area to participate in the restructuring of early childhood education. The new structure was based on a committee
composed of community people, teachers, and parents and was
the beginning of community organization and parental participation in early childhood education.

It was one of the aspects I've always looked for in a work
situation, [that is] there aren't any boundaries between
work and [the outside] social world. I saw a lot when I was
traveling in Third World countries and those distinctions
didn't exist there. And in this school [where she then
taught kindergarten], I developed my best friends [some of
whom are, twenty-five years later, still her best friends].
And we would do things like hang around school until
7 P.M. on Friday night, talking about what we were going to
do next week.

One time I remember we rented a cabin up in the gold
rush country the week after school was out [in order] to
work on materials that we hadn't gotten around to during
the school year. And no one paid us for that. It was a wonderful sense of accomplishment. There was real commitment
about what we were doing; it wasn't like, you know, you're
out the door at 5 P.M. And that was very important to me. The
sense of involvement. Also, the idea that we were sort of pio-
neers in this thing, and we were leading the way and other
people were going to follow and it was an improvement in
education. All of these things [were very important].

This situation represented many hours of overtime that Toni and her friends were neither paid for nor ever thought of being paid for. Rather, this volunteered time stemmed from their involvement and dedication to their work. Unfortunately, this sense of excitement, commitment, and community is lacking in Toni's current job. Part of this can be accounted for in terms of historical context—the innovative state and federal programs in education characteristic of the 1960s versus the noninvolvement or outright abandonment of education in the 1980s and 1990s. But another factor figures prominently as well. Toni currently works under the constraints of an all-encompassing federal bureaucracy. In the teaching job described earlier she did not. We will see how this difference made it difficult for her to enjoy being a child care administrator.

Toni worked in the same school district for seven and a half years (from about 1968–75). In 1975, she took a leave of absence from her job and traveled around the world for a year. While glad that she took the time to travel, she found herself in Berlin in 1976, feeling very much "at sea." As she put it, "you are what you do. If you do nothing (that is, are not working), you are nothing":

> I define myself in part by my work situation and when I first came here [to Berlin] there was no work situation and I didn't know how I was going to end up in anything that was related to work. And I was feeling very kind of diminished by that . . . less financially than in terms of "who am I?" If I don't have this thing called work, what am I going to do?

But here, as elsewhere, Toni proved to be resourceful. She was listening to the American radio station one day (she did not speak German) and heard an advertisement for teachers at a preschool operated by a parent board of directors, who were mostly Americans, that received logistical support from the army. She applied for and got the job on the basis of her past experience as a kindergarten teacher. Having done so, she almost immediately set about "organizing the school in a better fashion." The school was actually a large house, which gave it a "homey" environment. The teachers, most of whom were spouses of U.S. military personnel, were well meaning but not very professional. Their jobs provided them with a second income and something to do. The director's and staff's professional training were minimal, as were their salaries.

Toni set about correcting both of these problems. As was frequently the case, shortly after she got the job "a very strange thing happened." Over a period of three weeks, the director got divorced and moved back to the United States. At that point, the parent committee met and asked Toni to become the new director of the preschool. This represented a big change, since it catapulted her from a staff position to an administrative position for the first time. It was also something she looked forward to, since she felt that she could make a greater impact on restructuring the school as a director than as a teacher. And she was right. During her stay (1976–79) she increased the enrollment substantially, made more efficient use of space, increased the number of sessions taught, and increased the fees paid. This raised the school's income, some of which filtered down in the form of doubling teacher salaries, as well as increasing the school's ability to hire more competent and professional teachers.

From this child care center, Toni moved in 1980 to another operated by the army in Berlin. This occurred in the following way. The General Accounting Office (GAO), a governmental watchdog agency monitoring programs, wrote a scathing (and very embarrassing to the government) report on the poor quality of army-run child care facilities. This generated all sorts of plans designed to improve matters. In keeping with these efforts, an organization called Child Development Services was formed to serve as the administrative arm in charge of rectifying the gross deficiencies found to exist in government-run child care services. A new position was established for the person who would take charge on the local level—child development services co-ordinator. Toni wanted that job and made a conscious political effort to get it. Although she was not a family member of a child attending the center or married to someone in the military, which gave her the lowest possible priority rating, Toni eventually got the job. She was lucky she did, since becoming a candidate for the second job meant that she had to resign her position with the first. For her, it was all or nothing—new co-ordinator or unemployed. Being a risk taker, she took the gamble and won. She retained this position from 1980 to 1990. During this ten-year period, she initiated a number of novel changes in child care at her facility and others. She also raised the enrollment from 70 children to 300 and expanded the preschool facilities from a child care center in the basement of a skid row hotel to a new modern facility, the first of its kind built by the army. In 1990, she returned to the United States where she quickly acquired her current position of child development services co-ordinator on a U.S. military base.

We have followed Toni's career and shown how through luck, pluck, talent, and industry she moved from teaching to administration—from kindergarten teacher to child care services co-ordinator, and how her interests moved from hands-on teaching to student program development and teacher training. We will now consider some of the disadvantages that Toni experienced during her successful rise up the civil service ladder.

COPING WITH BUREAUCRACY: ON-THE-JOB FRUSTRATION AND ALIENATION

As a child care administrator, Toni describes the worst single feature of her work as follows:

> Well, one of the things I didn't like about it [working for the army as a civilian] was the constant fight with bureaucracy. It always seemed we were dealing with layers and layers of paperwork to get a supply order through or a sand box filled. I mean, you just couldn't pick up a phone and make it happen. . . . So you had to kind of develop a game mentality about it: "How can I beat this system." And it gets to be almost a challenge. You begin to get satisfaction for beating the system and making it work and at the same time thinking, "Why am I spending my time with this kind of junk?" It's a stupid thing to feel pride about; [for example] getting another $10,000 out of a general or something like that. One time, I remember we were at a huge meeting with all this brass, sitting around this huge mahogany table doing big budget stuff, hundreds of thousands of dollars here and there, and I—the child care center—beat out something like 100 binoculars for some troop unit [for an allocation]. I mean, that was a major victory (laughs).

She goes on to note that in any major organization, upper management people can't do all the work or be in total control. They have to allocate tasks to others. This means "convincing other people, training other people, supervising other people. What is your leadership effectiveness [if you have to go through convoluted bureaucratic channels on every routine occasion to accomplish these goals]?" When asked, "which is the bigger problem, managing people or contending with the ubiquitous constraints of bureaucracy," Toni felt the latter was definitely the greater challenge: "I think of bureaucracy with its annoying rules and regulations [as more difficult to contend with] than the direct supervision of staff."

The frustration generated by the constraints of bureaucratic chains of command is graphically illustrated in the following transcribed excerpt. It goes beyond the usual discrepancy between the real and the ideal routinely encountered in work settings.

> I talked to program directors, who then talked to their caregivers, who then talked to their caregivers, and so on. And this was hard and sometimes frustrating because I had a head full of all these wonderful concepts and ideas of what we should be doing for the kids, and I'd walk into the classroom and not see it happening. And then trying to figure out why not, and how do we get it there, and feeling the discrepancy between . . . my ideal and what actually was. And that was a problem for me. How do I bridge the gap between what I think should be and what actually is?

In describing her job in a nutshell, Toni put it this way:

> I still see it in the same way [as the co-ordinator job she held in Berlin]. I'm the person that organizes the resources and fights for funding and staff positions and staff autonomy and keeps those higher-level people from telling us how to operate things on the ground level. That's [part of the job] from me on up. Then from me down, it's all the ideas that are important about child care and the kids and early childhood and development—how do you get that happening in the classroom, again operating through at least two or three layers of staff. How do you convey these things, train people,

establish policies, and get these policies implemented. That's essentially what the job is.

The programs that resulted from these efforts were designed to serve children from four weeks to twelve years of age. In addition to designing and implementing child care programs for these children, Toni was also responsible for training and certifying caregivers (usually women) who provided care for children in their homes. All of these women lived on the military base in government housing. About half of the staff at the child care center were spouses of military personnel who lived on the base, and the other half lived off base in the local community. Which of these two categories of staff made the better child care workers is difficult to say. Those associated with military personnel were useful because they knew the system and how to work it. Toni, however, described this group as "inbred," while those from off base helped moderate the effects of "inbreeding."

Some indication of the level of inefficiency in the system, and how it subverted any effort to get things done can be gleaned from the following excerpt:

Toni: Well, one of the things I have to do is order supplies—toys, books, rattles, puzzles, whatever. And my system is I go through a catalog and I put yellow stickies on the things I want to order and the pages I want to order from, and I give them to the typist. The typist sits down and types this out, maybe comes up with four or five pages of items. And then that goes to the next office, and in that office, they retype it on the form they use in that office. Then from that office it goes to another office where it gets entered into a computer, so someone else is typing it again. From that office it goes to another office, where it's typed yet again into another computerized data bank. By now, it's been typed four times—this same four or five pages of information . . . and you have this [computer program] and I've got a different one. So the computers can't talk to each other.

I: Do you have anything like E-mail? You know, you type something on your computer that can be read on anyone else's, somewhere else, and you avoid a lot of paperwork.

Toni: I know what you mean. The higher-level people have that. I don't. And that works pretty well [for those who have it], not only by reducing paperwork, but because memos and letters typed on the computer don't have to conform to strict formal standards. That saves time and effort too.

Since all requests must be put in writing and typed according to strict formal criteria and sent to the correct offices for processing, competent secretarial help is essential if anything is to get done. Unfortunately, only upper-echelon military personnel get competent help. The level (in terms of federal civil service ranks, which translates into levels of competence) at which one can hire a secretary is contingent on one's own rank. Generals get high-ranked, competent secretarial assistance; Toni gets very low. This problem is compounded by the fact that high-ranked secretaries are well paid and stay put. Low-level secretaries are not only less competent but, after an initial ninety-day trial period, can and do apply for higher ranked, better paying positions. This leads to a low level of competence and a high level of mobility for the help Toni is eligible to recruit. The consequences of these policies for any formal organizational assessment of Toni's administrative efficiency is painfully obvious. Not only is it difficult to hire and retain a competent secretary, but it is even harder to fire one that is incompetent. Toni initiated dismissal proceedings against her secretary (after trying every other avenue of accommodation), and after almost nine months, the secretary was still "on her way out." Is it better to continue with incompetent help or risk having none at all? This question is apart from another that asks whether it is better to plod on, or spend the time and effort to be rid of one incompetent employee and train another one you can only hope is a part of your "vision." All of this tests not only one's administrative skills but one's therapeutic skills as well. One needs to exercise a great deal of patience and tact.

Yeah, you're the director, but you're always caught between [a rock and a hard place]. Do you fire this person, let this person go when you don't have enough people to take care of the children? Or, do you struggle and try to make it work and maybe it will change. And then there are the decisions

about when you've gone far enough with someone. Give it
your best but at some point you just have to say, "I'm not
investing any more time in this person. It's not going to get
any better. Pull out and start over again" . . . and then on top
of that, it's not so easy either [to fire someone even with
good cause] because there are regulations about notifica-
tions, time on the job, documenting and allowing time for
improvement, providing additional training, and all that . . .
so it's not so easy.

In addition to the frustration stemming from bureaucratic constraints, there were a number of other job-related features that
Toni disliked about her current employment. For example, she
didn't like the rush-hour commute, the lack of a sense of community she experienced at the child care center, the excessive and
unnecessary paperwork, the sense of increasing separation from
the children, too much time and effort spent on staff matters
(adults) and too little on the children in care, and, finally, the feeling of a progressive separation from professional peer group associations. These complaints made Toni's current job seem less
desirable than her first teaching jobs or her second administrative
position in Berlin.

It's very different to come into a program at the top and
[think] you're going to make changes and do all these great
things and find there is a kind of resistance and resentment to
whatever [you do]. Whereas in Berlin [and on her first teaching job] I grew with the program. The program started out
small [was less subject to the constraints of big bureaucracy].
It didn't have the same [level] of stratification that seems to
be in this job. Like in this job, somehow I have to maintain a
distance and am put at a distance. And that didn't seem to be
such a factor in Berlin. And it's a part of the job that I don't
like because what happens is that I don't have the same personal satisfaction from the job [that comes from] the connect-
edness with the people. . . . Even among my peers [in her
current job] there isn't a whole lot of social interaction.
I: If you don't have much interaction with your peers, do
you think they have much among themselves?

Toni: No, no . . . the thing that I call a sense of community in the workplace doesn't seem to exist overall, and I think it might be one of the reasons everything feels like such a struggle. You know, we don't help each other a whole lot. They are always building difficulties to overcome instead of making it easier for each other.

This nine-to-five mentality was something that Toni had trouble adjusting to, since it was contrary to most of her prior work experience. She also considered it unprofessional and selfish.

If it doesn't feel like you're working on something together, then something is missing in it for me . . . there's no proverbial "shared vision." And, for example, in my last job [in Berlin] and like I said in [her first job teaching the fifth and sixth graders and kindergarten] we would hang around a lot, you know, after work and talk about things. And everyone wasn't rushing out the door. Here, everyone counts [hours and effort]. I mean for overtime, for a half an hour— these are professional positions! And I'm not used to this nine-to-five mentality about a job. A couple of times I've suggested [unsuccessfully], "Why don't we get together over the weekend and knock out some of this stuff that's been hanging over us." People don't do that.

THE JOB VS. THE JOB DESCRIPTION

I: So, what do you think is the goodness of fit between the job you accepted ten months ago, as represented in your job description, and the job you actually found yourself doing?
Toni: Maybe it was 50 percent accurate. The real job is organizing services for children. That's the job that's on paper. But the real work is spinning wheels and pushing hard and overcoming resistance to doing what it is that you're supposed to be doing. And maybe it's that way in a lot of jobs but in this particular structure, it's particularly hard. You know, even in the smallest child care centers, where you are immediately involved in it [and don't suffer a sense of detachment as she does in her current job] you still spend

your time fixing the dishwasher, finding another cook, or the sprinkler system goes out. So, what's the real work there? But in this bureaucracy, I think it's even more cumbersome. You just spend a lot of time answering questions and responding to things that have nothing to do with the real work at hand. And then people wonder why the program isn't better than what it is. *And so you're sort of beat up for not doing what you should be doing because the system is preventing you from doing it.* [emphasis added]

As Toni sees it, it was not the regulations themselves that were evil, but the fact that they took on a "life of their own," and as they became more numerous and overly detailed, they became increasingly counterproductive.

It's like we created some kind of unmanageable monster. And you know my initial feeling about regulations was "This is a good thing. It gives you teeth to fight for what you need for the kids. It authorizes you to do the right thing for the children." But, it's become too detailed. You could never achieve the perfection [as it's given] in all this regulation stuff . . . and it's very demoralizing . . . it's like always grabbing [a thing that's] going out, and you can never quite pull it all back in. Kind of like constantly trying to get a handle [on it] . . . rein on it. I guess that's the word I want.
I: Like you're always rolling a big stone uphill?
Toni: That's right. That's right. In fact, someone gave me a Christmas card that was a big snowball being pushed uphill and the idea was, "We're going to get there somehow." But, to me it looked like this thing is gonna come right back down on me again (laughs). So, where are we with work [and getting things done]?

NECESSARY AND UNNECESSARY FORMS OF TRIVIA

In trying to show the various ways in which her job is composed primarily of unnecessary trivia in the form of symbolic correctness, Toni offers the following examples:

I still have a hard time understanding why I should take half an hour to an hour to produce this written memo when I can pick up the phone and talk about it in five minutes—maybe ten. And it gets even worse in the bureaucracy I work in because *format is everything* [emphasis added]. We have this correspondence, and it all has to be in the proper format. And if letters aren't lined up under the eagle [the army logo at the top of their letterhead], and the margin is not this many inches from the side of the page, then it gets kicked back [to the sender]. And people are afraid to pass it up to higher levels [of command where it needs to go to get consideration and authorization] because if it gets up to the highest level and a typo is found, then it looks bad for everyone down [the chain of command]. In addition to communicating ideas with memos, we're communicating the way the memo looks. That becomes as important [as the substance]. So of the ten hours a week or so I spend in writing things, I would guess that half of it is substance and a good portion of it is garbage—getting it to look right.

An example of this misplaced fastidiousness and its organizational consequences follows:

Right now I need some extra manual labor. There's a system for doing that; it's called a "detail." And you get these guys [soldiers] to come and work for you for a while. There's a person who's responsible for doing this [arranging for and dispatching the detail]. He has the authority to do that. But I can't pick up the telephone and say "could you arrange for these five people, you know, pick your own time, for three days [work]." No, no, I have to send a memo that goes to my boss, he brings it up to his boss, and then it goes from bosses to bosses and then it goes down again. And if any of those bosses doesn't like the format, you know, the i's aren't dotted right, they kick it back down again, and we start all over. And that's just an absurd waste of time.

I: What if everything is perfect and all goes well, how long does it take for them to send the detail?

Toni: Oh, that's one of the bad parts about it. I'm constantly underestimating how long it will take to get a piece of paper like that through. Assuming everything went right, like you said, it could take a week and a half.

I: What other things take time?

Toni: The other thing that interferes with the whole business is what we call "tracking." You don't know for sure that it [the memo] went from place *a* to *b* to *c* to *d* to *e* [through the proper chain of command], so you call *b*. "Yep, we got it"; "No, I don't remember seeing that"; "Gosh, I don't know what you're talking about"; or "Yeah, I saw it, we passed it on yesterday." So you call point *c* and make sure it got to point *d* [and so on]. . . .

And then to circumvent the whole mail system, we have a thing called "hand carry." Someone takes the time to move it personally from one office to the next office when a phone call would do.

I: Is there any way to beat the system?

Toni: Yeah. My last boss—I have a new one now—was trying to beat that system. He sent down a "directorate" that said "I don't want to see all this paper stuff. Just pick up the telephone and make things happen that way. Just handwrite something on a piece of paper. We don't want to waste time being paper pushers around here." Which was wonderful. But, he didn't make a dent in the system. Everyone was so used to sending memos, they couldn't stop.

Another example of the operation of the memo mill and how it helped subvert the possibility of solving the problems addressed is as follows:

You have an inspection [by your superiors whose job it is to monitor and assess the success of your program]. They come from all over the place and there must be three or four of these major inspections every year. [The inspectors write] inspection notices called "deficiencies of noncompliance," all of which are no secret to me. I know these "deficiencies" are there because I haven't gotten around to doing them: We don't have enough supplies; we don't have enough staff; we don't have enough time—that's how it is. Then, I have to spend days writing out a response to each of these things. "What's your corrective action plan" or "what's the progress of your corrective action plan," instead of making the corrections I'm writing about in the memo.

The time, effort, and attention that this bureaucratically generated minutiae required has effectively alienated Toni from the work she loves and the people she loves to work with and for.

I: What are some of the things you like and not like about your job?
Toni: What I think I like about it is the sense of potential. That's the idea that I've got this raw thing that's kind of a mess and if I keep working at it long enough and apply enough skill and vision and persistence, we're eventually going to build it up to something. The part of that that bothers me now is that I don't even think about the kids anymore. I just think about making the system work. And I hope that in the end is going to affect the kids. But part of it [the problem] is that my office is no longer located in the building where the children are, so I'm physically removed [from them] and it bothers me that there are some days where I don't see kids and hardly even think about kids. I think about adults and supervision and requirements and responding to memos.

We can see how Toni is not just physically separated from the children but how she has become progressively separated from what she believes ought to be the essential features of her job because of the time and attention the system requires her to give to the unessential features of her job. What's more, she is intelligent enough to recognize this, and it has given her second thoughts about pursuing her career, given where the pursuit of upward mobility would likely lead.

That's something that makes me think about how far I would want to go [up the career ladder]. I've been offered jobs at higher headquarter levels, but I don't think I could do

that [take a higher-echelon job] because all you are doing
then is paper stuff. . . . I certainly don't want to go back to
being in the classroom because I want a broader influence
than that, but there's a certain spot that's optimal [gives you
both some administrative influence and involvement with
the children]. And when you move too far away from it [up
the civil service ladder] you lose both.

We can glean from all this that it is not trivia per se that is bad in
Toni's eyes. Trivia that is related to and helps the children and
must be done is fine—necessary trivia that is part of our everyday
lives, such as cleaning the dishes and taking out the garbage. Even
in centers where the child care director has more control and is
subject to fewer bureaucratic constraints, there is still the dishwasher to fix, a cook to hire, or a sprinkler system that fails. Such
problems are seen as part of the territory. But, the senseless, endless, and redundant paperwork and rules and regulations that
contribute nothing to the working of the center, implementation of
programs, or training of teachers, Toni viewed as meaningless
trivia or "garbage." What's more, she estimated spending about
half of her on-the-job time on "garbage."

Whether on an individual or societal level, we are becoming
increasingly aware of the importance of getting rid of garbage.
Current political rhetoric states that in order to compete in "the
world marketplace," we need to become more competitive. To do
so, we need to dramatically increase efficiency, quality, and productivity. This book suggests in no uncertain terms that to do this
we need to reduce our output of garbage, that is, reduce the ubiquitous effects of bureaucratic constraints in the workplace.

CAREERS AS SERENDIPITOUS FINDINGS

Schwartz and Jacobs (1979:202–03) in paraphrasing Schutz's
(1967) observations note that

work [was] at the core of what everyday life was all about. In
work there is some project, some goal, known to the doer,
into which his actions fit as steps, means, or mini-ends in
themselves. This can be true of fixing a car, composing music

or selecting and getting to a movie. As a scheme of interpretation, "the job and its accomplishment" provides a way to structure the meaning of all acts occurring in connection with it. Most of our fact finding and reasoning within daily life have a practical, and not theoretical motive. The motive is the mastery and manipulation of the world so as to realize our various aims. All this can be summarized thus: We chronically assume about people, events, and happenings of daily life that we can be affected by them and can affect them in eminently practical ways. Because of this, we are anything but disinterested observers of this world. Its events and happenings are addressed with an eye to what they will do to us and what we can do to them.

This conscious rational effort to solve on-the-job practical problems as they arise in eminently practical ways has been highlighted in all of these case studies. Toni's effort to overcome the constraints of bureaucracy in the ways she did in order to accomplish her work, the way she set about getting (as well as doing) her job, what the army did to inhibit her efforts to achieve her ideals at the child care center, and how she routinely worked to circumvent these hurdles are examples of practical rational reasoning in everyday life to solve the problems that occur on and off the job. The preceding case studies have offered many examples of this practical reasoning and how it was used by Joan and Ann to solve the daily problems confronting them in their jobs.

There is, however, another element that runs concurrently with this process. In the process of solving one immediate practical problem confronting the individual on the job (or off it), one not infrequently creates or discovers another related but unanticipated problem that presents another challenge to practical reasoning and, at the same time, changes not only one's prior course of action but one's new intended goals. Viewed in this way, career paths can be seen as a succession of serendipitous encounters that one pursues or not, depending on one's changing "definition of the situation" (Thomas and Znaniecki, 1928) and one's assessment of it at any point in time. This is true not only for on-the-job decisions and the emerging career path that it produces, but of life in general and the life "career" (Goffman, 1959) that it produces.

If we allow that most of life is composed of a series of small, inconsequential, even trivial events, some of which confront us on a daily basis as immediate practical problems we are obliged to overcome, then we can see the nontrivial nature of trivia on and off the job, since it is the essence of work in particular and life in general. To some of these problems of everyday life, we attribute greater or lesser importance. We do this to give meaning to our actions and to our lives. If all problems were considered trivial, life would be boring, uninteresting, meaningless, and ultimately unliveable. If all problems were monumental and seemed insurmountable, life would be experienced as chronically taxing, overwhelming, and again, ultimately unliveable. In order to give interest and meaning to life, one attributes little importance or meaning to most problems and great importance and meaning to a smaller number of others. This results in a life full of "ups and downs" (Jacobs and Glassner, 1982). What's more, it results in a life of more (but smaller and unnoticed) "ups" and fewer but bigger and more profoundly felt "downs." This is the life most of us lead and find in an unreflective way to be normal and liveable. For some, the problem occurs when we experience more and larger "downs" than "ups," and when the "ups" are perceived of as so inconsequential and the "downs" so monumental, life becomes unbearable. People who experience such a life frequently reach "the end of hope" and suicide (Jacobs and Glassner, 1982). Viewed in this way, life requires from us a constant, sometimes heroic, effort to deal with an unending stream of little problems, so that they do not become big ones, while viewing the timely disposal of these little problems as a series of little victories. Simultaneously, we need to not become overwhelmed by big problems. This means that we need to find meaning in the routine trivia of everyday life and, at the same time, not be overwhelmed by atypical major problems infrequently encountered in the course of a lifetime. Seeing life, and the individuals in it in these terms, we can understand employment and life careers as a series of smaller or larger serendipitously encountered problems that we undertake to solve through practical reasoning. The kind of emergent career path or life line this produces for us is contingent on our success in solving immediate problems and (unforeseen) successive ones as they occur. Who will best succeed in this basic undertaking and why is difficult or impossible to predict. We can see how this unpredictability was played out over a twenty-year period in the lives of Joan, Ann, and Toni. None of them could have begun to successfully predict their employment careers. This was also true of those who knew them.

6

God Help the Needy: Fran, HIV Clinic Director

I started to write a book called *A Portrait of the Artist as a Housewife*. I wanted to write a collection of stories and vignettes about things like my toaster oven and my relationships with plumbers, mailmen and delivery people. But life dealt me a much more complicated story. On October 21, 1986, I was diagnosed with ovarian cancer. Suddenly I had to spend all my time getting well. I was fighting for my life against cancer. . . . The book has turned out a bit differently from what I intended. It's a book about illness, doctors and hospitals; about friends and family; about beliefs and hopes. It's about my life, especially about the last two years. And I hope it will help others who live in the world of medication and uncertainty. (Radner, 1990)

It is no accident that Gilda Radner found it relatively easy to write about her two-year battle with cancer, in view of Schutz's (1967) observation that our main concern in everyday life is the solution of practical problems in eminently practical ways. Greater problems command greater attention, and problems of life and death, such as cancer or AIDS, command our greatest attention and efforts. Major problems of this kind are unexpected, unwanted, and unusual and as such stand out as an undeniable and all-consuming part of our existence. They are easy to "see." Indeed, like a toothache when it occurs, it is difficult to experience anything else. Our attention is totally focused. On the other hand, toaster ovens and mailmen and delivery people (the trivia and stuff of everyday life) goes essentially unnoticed. "Seeing" and writing about these things is, as many social scientists have found, extremely difficult. If Radner had not been afflicted with ovarian cancer, it is unlikely she would have succeeded in writing the book she initially set out to write.

People suffering from AIDS have essentially the same experience as Radner. Their disease confronts them as an all-encompassing problem that requires all of their energy. Unlike Radner, however, most people with AIDS (98% of those in Fran's clinic) are "medically indigent adults." Such people, without medical coverage or with inadequate medical coverage, have to rely on state and federally funded support services. This puts them in double jeopardy. Suffering from an incurable disease, they have to deal with the critical questions of death and dying, while simultaneously searching for the medical and support services that sustain life. Regardless of circumstances, financial or otherwise, those dealing with serious illness proceed in the same fashion, with a step-by-step search for practical solutions to practical problems as they develop in the course of their disease. Radner's book *It's Always Something* graphically illustrates this. Even the title implies it. This helps us to understand how and why, as Fran tells us, the gay community became a political power that was able to embarrass the government to some extent into confronting the AIDS problem. In Fran's county there were between 4,000 and 6,000 suspected cases of HIV-positive people and about 300 patients with AIDS. According to Fran, these people "had no physicians that were willing to see any of them. And so they had to build a clinic"—the one she came to direct. In the case study that follows, we will consider why she had such a hard time establishing the clinic and why so many needy patients had a difficult time getting the type of assistance they needed from it.

CAREER PATH

In 1968 Fran graduated from nursing school, which was "a traditional three-year nursing school that existed in those days and is now almost nonexistent. At that time what you got was a diploma in nursing. The jobs I had for the next fifteen years or so were in intensive care units, coronary units, or emergency rooms."

Her first job was as a primary care provider in an intensive care unit. After two years, she married and moved to another city, state, and job, where she worked for a year in a coronary unit (about 1970–71). She moved again (following her husband and his career) and was employed for about four years as a pulmonary intensive care specialist. This was followed by a fourth move and a number of years working in intensive care and coronary units. Between 1974 and 1986, she went from staff nurse to either supervisor or director of intensive care or emergency room units or clinics. About 1986, due to an on-the-job injury, she could no longer do heavy work. From about 1986 to 1989, she worked part time in a physician's office and part time for the American Red Cross. Following this, she was employed for a year or so in a hospice. During this same period, she worked toward her bachelor's and master's degrees, which took a total of five years (1986–91). As Fran put it, "after three years of nursing school [attended on an eleven-month-a-year basis] and eighteen years of nursing experience, I was given a grand total of 30 units of college credit [toward her bachelor's degree]."

After receiving her master's degree as a family nurse practitioner with a clinical specialty in HIV work, she found her current job as director of HIV clinical services.

JOB SATISFACTION

In terms of pay, benefits, convenience, and feeling of collegiality with her peers, Fran felt that most of the nursing jobs she held were good most of the time, at least in the first half of her career.

And so, in the first ten or twelve years, yes, they [her jobs] were very challenging . . . but that was because of my age and the time [early in her career] that I enjoyed those jobs. As far as benefits and salary, and those kinds of things, I've always been well paid and the salaries and benefits have always been good. As far as convenience goes, I've always lived fairly close to where I worked.

I: How did you get along with the people you worked with?

Fran: Intensive care units, ERs, and coronary care units are very different than classic Med-Surge [medical-surgical] kinds of floors that nurses work on. Because the jobs are so challenging, highly specialized, and require so much specialized knowledge, they become very close knit family structures and very supportive.

For Fran, nursing has always seemed a good career choice in terms of salary and benefits, convenience, and peer support. If there was a problem, it occurred during the second half of her career and in an area regarding medical ethics and the intrinsic value of the work itself.

The problems for me was when I started dealing with issues of ethics and what I was doing. When you are working on these kinds of units, you often are involved in what I consider real questionable research protocols that are simply set up for the sake of research and have very little to do with necessary knowledge. That's especially true in university [medical research] centers.
I: So, it's like the protocols may have been good science, but they may not have been . . .
Fran: . . . good for the patients. No. No. The university system's highest priority is research first, second is teaching, and third, and very, very low priority, is the clients. The patients really have very, very little value other than [being] an entity to practice on. It's a very brutal system, actually.

This mid-career disenchantment with the system led Fran to change from hands-on clinical work to nursing administration.

BURNOUT AS A MOTIVATOR TO UPWARD MOBILITY

"Burnout" is generally understood to have a negative connotation. One who is burned out is someone who has become disenchanted, alienated (Seeman, 1959), blasé (Simmel, 1950), and generally lacking in motivation as a result of their continued exposure to a stressful and/or unrewarding job. Burned out people are those who are considered to be disinterested and/or incapable of any longer doing a good job. Such people might be expected to become downwardly mobile. The professional women studied in this book did not live up to this expectation. Indeed, an analysis of their career paths reveals just the opposite. Burnout was a direct cause of their move from hands-on staff work to administrative jobs and upward mobility.

For example, in Chapter 3, Joan, after twenty years of "getting nowhere" as a secretary was feeling burned out. At that point, she decided that she needed a change and applied for a job as publications specialist with a university. She felt that her new job would provide a more stimulating environment and more interesting work, as well as the greater potential for upward mobility and she was right. In the next seven years, she moved from an unchallenging staff position to an administrative position that enhanced her status and power, greatly improved her benefits, and tripled her salary.

In Chapter 4, Ann also moved up and into an administrative job because of the burnout she experienced in lower-echelon positions. The cause of burnout for these women varied, but the net result was that they became upwardly mobile. Ann, after three years as a half-time abortion counselor for Planned Parenthood (two as a volunteer, one as a paid employee), quit because of burnout and moved on to become a certified childhood educator in order to enter a less stressful line of work and one she enjoyed more.

In another job she experienced burnout, not because of the depressing or oppressive nature of the work, but because of the "insanity" of bureaucratic constraints (Jacobs, 1969). All of this moved her toward upward mobility in the search for some autonomy over the work she did. By becoming an administrator, she felt there was at least the promise of autonomy, and with this expectation in mind, she moved up the bureaucratic ladder.

In Chapter 5, Toni felt the need to leave the classroom for an administrative job in order to be better able to reform early childhood educational policies in preschool settings. She also hoped to overcome some of the constraints of bureaucracy by moving into a higher position within the bureaucracy. All of these women were frustrated in these efforts. They found themselves subject not to fewer constraints, but only to the dictates of different superiors and sets of constraints. As administrators, Joan, Ann, Toni, and Fran were able to enhance their status, increase their salaries (and levels of responsibility), and to some extent extend their autonomy. But all felt a widening gap between their new-found levels of responsibility and sense of professionalism and their actual levels of power and their ability to affect change.

While becoming administrators did not solve all of their problems, and some of these women became burned out administrators instead of burned out lower echelon staff, it was the hope of escaping from their earlier burned-out state that motivated all of them to move upward in their careers.

> *Fran*: Often what happens to nurses who no longer want to do the clinical type of work, you become an administrator, simply because it gets you away from the clinical work you are not satisfied with. So, it becomes an escape mechanism. A lot of nurses mumble and groan about how administration work takes them away from the bedside [or, for Toni, the classroom]. But my experience with most administrative nurses is that they didn't want to be there anymore anyhow. *Part of the problem with being a staff nurse or even a clinical specialist is that you have very little control over the environment that you work in.* [emphasis added]

Granted, there are different possible outcomes for those suffering burnout. Some may be fired for exhibiting an indifferent attitude or incompetent performance. Some may become fixed at a low-level job, which they are afraid to quit, and suffer in silence. Others, as was the case with the women in this study, may try to change their situation by moving up the career ladder. The choice of options taken, and their outcomes, are, in part, a function of one's level of risk taking and a variety of unknown and perhaps unknowable factors referred to earlier as serendipitous findings. In some cases, however, the desperation produced by burnout motivates people to take risks they might have otherwise avoided. These risk-taking efforts sometimes turn out well and lead to better jobs and upward mobility, or sometimes turn out poorly, that is, downward mobility and lower-status jobs. We need to recognize the possible positive effects of burnout and try to understand why it motivates some people to change and others not. We also need to understand the direction of change that burnout produces. In the current research, the study of the positive potential of burnout has been badly neglected.

THE EFFECTS OF BUREAUCRATIC CONSTRAINTS

Fran, like Toni, felt she was rolling a series of large boulders up a steep hill in her effort to make her clinic operational. The problems of bureaucracy were pervasive. For example, there was the billing issue.

> One of the biggest problems we had working with the state was to get medical reimbursement from the federal government so we could bill for our services because about 98 percent of our patients have no funding other than [state or federal] medical [coverage]. They are what's called CMSP, which is medically indigent adults. And these patients cannot receive care other than [what] the county system provides because private physicians won't take them because there is not enough reimbursement. The [bureaucratic] system is too much of a hassle [for the doctors and for her]. It took me close to seven months [of the ten months she has been director of the clinic] to get a medical provider number out of the state [without which the clinic could not operate since it could not bill]. I ended up with a file that was six inches thick. I believe the state doesn't want to give out a provider number because it doesn't want us to have a way of billing them. I can't explain it any other way.

The following is another example of Fran's distress with bureaucracy.

> It's very frustrating. The community on the outside saying "We have people dying. We have people dying. Why isn't this moving?" Bureaucracies never ever move quickly. You have to get all your little ducks in a row to make sure things [move] because if the ducks are not in a row, the bureaucracy

not only grinds to a halt, but it digs its heels in and won't move at all. And on the other side, you do the political thing and become a part of the old-boy network which is a part of bureaucracies. That [is] you pat a lot of heads, and you make sure that you do a favor for this person [and hope that the favor will be returned]. . . . As my secretary, who I very much appreciate, said, "If you want to change a county system [of bureaucracy], talk to God. If you want to get around a county system, find somebody who's worked it for awhile and knows the system." And that's the truth. You don't change the system

We have seen in the preceding chapters that Joan, Ann, and Toni ultimately came to the same realization. They all found themselves in positions of great responsibility but little power. A quote from Fran serves to illustrate this point.

You rapidly come to realize that in bureaucracy there are very few people that truly have any power at all. [In the county system] the power is in the board of supervisors. And so [to get things approved] you keep going up administrative levels. You have tremendous responsibility but really very little power to initiate actions. Everything has to go through level after level and finally gets approved or disapproved by the board of supervisors. So that was probably the biggest thing I had to realize was that, yes, I could write reports and make recommendations, and yes, if you are careful about getting your ducks in a row, in working the system, you get something done. But just because you are bright and have great ideas doesn't mean that what you want is going to get accomplished. It's all the other stuff [the "garbage" or the "politics"] that feeds into it. So, for me, I think the rudest awakening of the job, and as I talk to other managers they think the same, is the fact that the responsibility is there, but the power is not.

This feeling of "powerlessness" (Seeman, 1959) and the frustration and sense of futility that it produces can be seen in the following excerpt:

Fran: It's very frustrating. So why do I stay on this job? So why do I do this? Cause it's crazy. You know, why put up with all this crap? They pay me a lot of money, that's one reason [quick laugh]. The other is that it's a real challenge to develop something and to build something, and to put together something that is in your mind's eye of what should be. But whether a year from now we'll have it, I don't know.

Like Toni, Fran had a "vision" for which she put up with "all this crap." And, like Ann, her high salary was not the only motivating force behind her enthusiasm to realize that vision. Remember, Toni had turned down higher-echelon jobs that she felt would only increase her sense of "powerlessness" and "meaninglessness" (Seeman, 1959) and put her vision in jeopardy. This was true of Joan and Ann as well. The single most potent factor in producing a sense of frustration and creeping alienation in all of these professional women, employed in different settings and working at different jobs, was not pay or benefit issues but the ubiquitous untoward effects of bureaucracy.

PLAYING POLITICS

"Playing politics" refers in this context to the sense of frustration all of these women felt in having to mediate so many competing factions and interests in the course of carrying out the day-to-day requirements of their jobs. We have seen how as publications coordinator, Joan had to mediate and integrate the needs of her boss, those she supervised, the printers, designers, customers, and outside providers. Ann, the principal administrative analyst, had to worry about the interests of her boss, her secretary, the university, and the students. Toni, as child care administrator, also had to coordinate the interests of many competing factions: "the big brass," her secretary, the children, their parents, the staff, and outside child care providers. The efforts of these professional women playing politics in their respective jobs was seen by them as a necessary and sometimes challenging part of their work. They, however, also saw it as a part of their jobs that consumed most of their time and contributed least to the achievement of their goals. This was true in

Fran's case, as well. She was responsible for hiring a clinic doctor, a secretary, a benefits counselor, and a case manager who was a licensed clinical social worker. In addition to getting all these people to perform, managing an annual budget of $1.5 million, mediating intrastaff disputes and those between the staff and the community and/or herself, she also had to contend with the competing interests of outside community-based organizations.

> Probably 90 percent of my job is politics. HIV medicine is politically a very controversial thing and there's tremendous vested interest by the [gay] community to make sure that the clinics get up and running, and they're run well. So I often think that I'm on a tightrope between the county at one end, who's my employer, and the [gay] community, who are very politically astute and very active on the other side of the tightrope, who are demanding services. I walk the tightrope between the two and often both ends get frayed. You're not only on a tightrope but you're on an awful unstable end. So I spend a good deal of my time cajoling and trying to reach compromises between CBOs [community-based organizations], who do HIV work and are often at open warfare with each other [and the county]. And a lot of my job is simply getting people to sit down and talk about kinds of services and making them accessible to patients. Today, I spent six [hours] out of an eight-hour day doing politics and that's often the case.

All of this says nothing of the diplomatic tact needed to politically circumvent the constraints of bureaucracy and the counterproductive efforts of higher-echelon people within the organization. In Fran's case, what this model portrays is two or more powerful warring factions—the gay community and the county board of supervisors—who were often at odds with each other, and Fran (with very little power) caught in the middle mediating an endless string of disputes between the two. An organizational structure of this sort is likely to produce a bad case of burnout in a very short period of time.

Another illustration of this counterproductive situation was the clinic's need to hire (for the second time in ten months) a primary care physician. Normally, the hiring of a doctor in a clinical setting does not involve community participation. The community does not have a vote in the selection, since this is seen as a medical decision to be decided by the doctor-candidate, his or her peers, and the hospital or clinical administration. In the case of staffing Fran's clinic, this was not true. Community organizations felt they should have a vote in deciding which doctor got the job and why. The county board of supervisors and Fran thought otherwise, each for different reasons. The gay community felt that the clinic was a public service agency, and since they were primarily the ones being served, they wanted a voice in the selection process. The county board of supervisors thought this should be a medical and not a political decision. Fran, as the director of the clinic, also felt the selection of a staff physician should be a medical decision. Her position, however, involved not only the rational selection of the best available candidate based on medical qualifications, but one that met organizational requirements, as well. This was dictated by her vision of an HIV clinic that incorporated many, if not most, of the features found in the hospice model. Fran had previously worked in a hospice setting and was favorably impressed by the way it was organized, the dedication of those who worked there, and the level of care they were able to deliver. This commitment to the hospice model required Fran to find a capable doctor able to work within that model. She thought she had done that when she hired the clinic's first doctor, but she was mistaken. He proved to be a very capable practitioner and well versed in HIV treatment. From strictly a medical point of view, he would be hard to replace. Unfortunately, he was not a team player and wanted to be in total control, not only of his hours, salary, and patients, but of most other clinic decisions as well. This was, of course, what the director was hired to do, and Fran and the doctor became embroiled in a power struggle. For the doctor to acknowledge Fran as the director required a role reversal that he was incapable of making. It required the doctor to take orders from the nurse director. Generally, doctors are unaccustomed to taking orders from nurses, but they are accustomed to giving nurses orders that they expect to have followed without question. Fran's firing of her first staff physician took about as long as it took Toni to get rid of her inherited secretary—about seven months.

The second doctor was a person who was much more agreeable and accommodating, not only to Fran, but to the rest of the clinic staff, as well. While he was not a better doctor than the first one, he was capable and helped to get the clinic up and running, something that the first doctor, despite his high level of medical competence, could not do. Constantly mediating disputes between all of these interest groups took its toll on Fran:

> The new physician, after he sat through four hours of political meetings just shook his head and said, "Why don't they just get off your back and let you build the clinic?" [I said] "Because it's not that simple. You spend a lot of time compromising to the point where you get a product probably nobody's happy with . . . one of the things about being a bureaucrat that's managing a system is that you make lots of compromises and a lot of times you don't remember where you started before you compromised, or even what the goal was."

MEANINGFUL WORK

In the preceding chapter, we saw how Toni tried to strike a delicate balance between doing what she perceived as meaningful work—work that involved her directly with the children and their problems—and administrative bureaucratic work that alienated her from the children. If one went too far up the administrative ladder, one dealt only in paperwork, a form of work that held little meaning. On the other hand, if one stayed only in the classroom in lower-echelon jobs, the work was more meaningful but one lost salary, status, autonomy, and what little power or chance one might have to help the children indirectly by bringing about policy changes. It was generally believed that somewhere in between was the best possible compromise for achieving meaningful work and accomplishing one's employment and personal goals.

Fran experienced the same dilemma. The call for hands-off people and hands-on paper was a major requirement of the job for all of these women. Because of this, they all sought elsewhere to find meaning in their work. Since it was not to be found in "shuffling papers," they found it instead in the direct contact with the people they worked with and/or for. This helped all of them to maintain their sanity in the face of work they otherwise described as crazy, meaningless, unproductive, bureaucratic paper or people work. The following is an example of Fran's on-the-job search for the meaning as the director of the HIV clinic.

> I'm going to spend more time in the clinic even though I don't have the time. It's just for my sanity. It's also better for the patients for me to be there because then they have another person other than the doc [to talk to]. But you know, today, I saw only two patients in the clinic. One of them was a twenty-two-year-old girl who probably was infected when she was fifteen or sixteen years old. I'm dealing with a twenty-two-year-old girl, and she is dealing with the fact that she has a terminal disease. She's already quite sick. Her T-cells are quite low. The chances of her having a significant opportunistic infection, one of the bad ones associated with AIDS, within the next year are pretty high. And she would much rather be shopping at Macy's than sitting in a clinic talking to me about having a tubal ligation at twenty-two years old. You know, she has a disease that can be transmitted to her infant. And today she was saying to me, "I want to be sterilized." And I'm saying to her, "That's a big decision, you're twenty-two now, and in five years"—um, she won't be alive in five years—but if she was [because] say something happened in research that she was alive in five years and we found something that would prevent her transmitting her virus to her offspring, "maybe we need to talk [about] different methods of birth control."

The patient went on to tell Fran how she was just fired from her job when her boss learned that she was HIV positive.

> So, now we have economic issues as well. We have death and dying issues. I mean, how many twenty-two year olds have to deal with death and dying issues? She needs a support system. She needs groups to talk to. She needs to learn about her disease—how to manage it. We have to be able to

work with this kid so that she is strong enough to be able to tell her parents—which she has not done. Her parents don't know. There are three people in the whole world that know this lady is HIV positive and two of them are myself and the doctor. The other is her boss. She is totally isolated. That is not a problem that one person can look at and solve. . . .

The best-case scenario, and that's the whole reason I spend so much time doing politics, is to get people to the point where they see that their vested interest is the client and not their agency. First of all, they need to see that they are not providers of care [but] facilitators of care, and they don't manage people; they facilitate services. The ultimate manager has to be the client himself. And so the system has to do a great deal of letting go of power, which a lot of people have a great deal of trouble doing. Certainly our medical establishment isn't set up that way.

Working directly with the clients in the clinic for about eight hours a week not only helped Fran to "maintain her sanity" and find meaning in her work, it also helped her to establish the clinic on a hospice model.

MEANINGLESS WORK

If working directly with patients for eight hours a week in the clinic was a meaningful part of Fran's work, the two or three hours of paperwork associated with those contacts were seen as less than meaningful. Fran also spent about fifteen hours a week on the phone, most of it "doing politics"; twelve to sixteen hours a week in meetings generating policy; perhaps seven hours a week dictating memos; and four hours a week doing budget, paying bills, and "tracking" (a process described in the preceding chapter by Toni who spent even more time than Fran on "tracking"). Finally, about an hour or less a week was spent on "education," teaching a class on HIV-related issues. In all but the last of these activities, the bulk of the day-to-day requirements of the job were seen as essentially meaningless work. What made them meaningless was that they consumed most of one's time and effort on the job and contributed little or nothing to helping needy patients or to getting the clinic organized and operational. The result of these activities produced in Fran a growing sense of frustration and alienation, which culminated in a sense of futility and low job satisfaction. This in turn led to low morale and motivation and the decreasing prospect of ever fulfilling the avowed goals of the agency as described in the official job description.

If this was so for a group of capable and highly motivated women, all of whom managed in a competitive field to rise to middle- or high-level administrative positions, imagine the effects of bureaucratic constraints on the job performance of the less educated and motivated workers who compose the bulk of the American workforce. Given that most work settings are to a greater or lesser extent bureaucratically organized and managed, it is remarkable that they are able to function at all in the competitive marketplace of global economics. Indeed, it is becoming increasingly clear that the United States is on a downward spiral in this regard. Other countries have initiated management models that have increased productivity, if not job satisfaction. What is needed is a form of management and organizational structure that enhances both.

ADMINISTRATIVE SKILLS

Fran was hired to create and administer a county AIDS clinic with a budget of $1.5 million. Needless to say, this was a very responsible job that would require not only a great deal of administrative skill but extensive knowledge on a wide range of topics. Where and how did Fran acquire these skills? It would seem reasonable to suppose that at least some of these administrative skills were a product of her eight years of combined higher education. In the course of acquiring a master's degree as a nurse practitioner, she probably learned a great deal about nursing administration.

> *I*: You do budgets and billings, draw up contracts, teach classes on HIV-related topics, mediate political disputes, train and organize staff, etc. Where did you learn to do all that? Was it a part of your nursing curriculum?
> *Fran*: No . . . they taught us nothing about management or budget. The clinical work, yes, but not the rest.

I: Well, how did you learn to do the rest?

Fran: You keep a checkbook for awhile. . . .

I: I keep a checkbook but I could never manage a million and a half dollars budget.

Fran: You learn as you go along. I think one of the things that most people don't realize is that any nursing job that has any supervisory or administrative stuff attached to it [as her earlier jobs did] does all these things. Nurses for years have been involved with programs very similar [to the one she is now administrating] so that people skills and management skills that I learned when I managed intensive care units, and coronary care or ERs, you know, you just kind of move [this knowledge and skill] from one place to another. . . .

When they hired me to do this job, they would not have hired somebody fresh out of a master's program who had just become a nurse practitioner to do this job. They hired someone who had years of administrative background. That's what they were looking for. But they also need the credentials because anytime you write a job description you write the credentials on top of what you need. And it was written for a clinical nurse practitioner with HIV specialty because they knew that whoever was hired had to be able to work with private docs, occasionally see patients, and handle community stuff. But the thing [they most wanted] was real firm administrative skills. They hired an administrator far more than they hired a clinician. Clinicians are easy to come by. Administrators aren't. And that's what we are learning with our docs [the ones the clinic hired]. The doc who just left was a superb clinician, but he knew nothing about systems or how to make things work. So [administration] is an accumulated bunch of skills that you learn over years and it's not taught. But it should be. Any nurse who has a bachelor's degree now is going to be in some level of management. If you have a master's degree, you're definitely going to be in management. You can get a [special] master's degree in nursing administration, but it [administration] needs to be more integrated into all nursing programs. Whether it's a clinic or hospital, nurse practitioners are going to end up [being] managers.

I: What do you think is the "goodness of fit" between your job description—what you thought you would be doing—and what you actually ended up doing?

Fran: The real good news is that we have a real shot at developing something that is very, very different from what normally occurs, and that's a partnership between a county and a community-based structure. It requires a lot of interest by all the players, and I think it is really there. There's a lot of headaches getting to that point but I think the basic desire in all the groups is there. That's the real good part [of the job] and that's why I keep doing it. If one meeting fails, you try another meeting and you keep going further [ahead] each time. If something politically falls apart, you figure out how to take care of it.

I: Is there a downside to the job?

Fran: It's not the people who work with me or below me [that is a problem]. It's the upper echelon of the county [the board of supervisors who have all the power and ultimately makes all the major and some minor decisions]. That's the problem in any county system. [I] have no control whatsoever [over that]. Bureaucrats don't want to change things. "If it works, you don't want to fix it." When you're building a clinic and there's no clinical services in the county, you're obviously coming up against change. You know, you run into a lot of walls on that, you really do. I think that one of the things that surprised me most was how entrenched bureaucracies can be.

Another frustrating feature of the job, in addition to bureaucracy's inability to overcome inertia, was the lack of power Fran, as the director, felt she had to effect the necessary changes to make the clinic a success.

Again, I have a lot of responsibility, but I don't have a lot of power. People say bureaucratic systems are bad. I don't know if this one is particularly bad [but] county government is very autocratic and like many autocratic systems they don't ask for a lot of input from folks below them. So, I will write a budget and say, "We need x amount of money." But what often happens is on a unilateral basis people [the county board of supervisors] will change my budget. It will come back down, and they have moved it [the items in the budget] all around. And I have very little input on what got moved [to where or why].

The other thing that is *really* frustrating is that because it is civil service, you have limited ability to hire who you want to hire. It's done on seniorities. The county is now going through layoffs and any of the jobs that are available in the clinic have to be offered first to people who have been laid off. . . . Sure, I have a big budget, and to a certain extent, I have discretion on how it's spent, but it really is not that simple. I don't have a checkbook . . . [the county board of supervisors does].

In a formal sense, we can see that the jobs of these professional women have much in common. On the positive side, each had in their own domain a vision of what they hoped to accomplish. Initially, they believed that if they could not accomplish everything, they could at least achieve a good segment of it. On the negative side, we have seen how this early enthusiasm later changed to cautious optimism and finally gave way to despair over ever bringing about real change within the system. We have seen, through a case study analysis, how and why this state of affairs came to pass and some of the changes that would be necessary at managerial, organizational, and worker levels to improve matters. Not all of these women suffered the same level of burnout or disenchantment with bureaucracy. Ann and Fran probably experienced more of both; Joan and Toni experienced less. Still, the negative impact of bureaucracy on all of the women was striking. This problem is not restricted to professional women. Professional men suffer the same complaints. A prime example is a man who works as an AIDS researcher in the South Bronx. He had worked in this position for two years, when asked how his job was going. One would expect to hear about the depressing nature of his work with terminally ill patients, the hazards of working on the streets of the South Bronx, and the problems of finding affordable housing in New York City. "The job's pretty terrible," he said. When asked about the terminally ill, the hazards of street work, the tough neighborhood, and the poor housing, he said, "No, no—it's not that. It's the fucking bureaucracy that's driving me crazy." The work, the pay, and the benefits were not the problem. It was the bureaucratic organization of his agency that made his life difficult and the work impossible. We will see how this finding is consistent with our final case study of Freda, a licensed clinical psychologist.

7

Public and Private Practice: Freda, Clinical Psychologist

> Every morning when we wake we confront a familiar world. Considering the day ahead we mark off that which might be pleasurable from that which will produce anxiety, irritation, boredom or depression. Each day's living constitutes a series of projects in which we either accept the arrangements that await us, or attempt to manipulate them, so that they will be more amenable, more compatible with the view we hold of ourselves. In this book we will talk about how people make out in their world, the whimsical, pathetic, outrageous ways in which they manipulate its demands. (Cohen and Taylor, 1978:10)

Before outlining Freda's educational and occupational career path, we should explore how she came to choose psychology in the first place. Like all of the women in this study, her current career was a product of the inexorable law of "one thing leads to another." In short, Freda becoming a psychologist was the result of "drift" (Matza, 1964).

> I: Look, it's unlikely you sprung from the womb thinking "I'll be a psychologist." How did you get interested in psychology in the first place?

Freda: Well, I was always interested in things that people do, like thinking and remembering. All of that fascinated me. Things that go on in your head that really can't be measured too effectively. To study this, I wanted to go into biology. I had this wonderful professor as an undergraduate, who essentially told me that biology is not developed anywhere near the point where the questions I had would ever be answered and if I was interested in these things I should go into psychology. So I did. I think that had a big influence.

Another aspect that influenced her decision to become a psychologist was more personal:

I think the other thing was that I was in therapy myself as a child and it helped me a great deal, and so I was very interested in that. You know, it made quite an impression on me.

CAREER PATH

Primarily as a result of these two chance occurrences, Freda became a psychologist. In 1964 she received her Ph.D. in clinical psychology from a major university. Her first job was with a county health program, a position that she held for thirteen years (1965–78). Following this, she worked half time for seven years in a private clinic and half time in private practice (from about 1978–85). From 1985 until the time of this interview in 1991, Freda was in private practice full time as a clinical psychologist. Her work career as a psychologist spanned a total of twenty-seven years. Roughly half of this was in private clinical practice and half in the public sphere.

PUBLIC VS. PRIVATE PRACTICE

In a retrospective analysis of her career, Freda concluded that she was much happier in private practice than when she was employed as a clinical psychologist with the county. It should be noted that there was an early and later period to her county job. The early period (from about 1965 to 1972) she found enjoyable:

> When I was first hired I was involved in starting a new unit and that was actually quite enjoyable and interesting. I would say that my experiences in working with these people was quite good.

After about seven years she was transferred to another county unit, and her job satisfaction level dropped precipitously.

> When I transferred, I was given assurance about how the job would go. Then it turned out that two new administrators were hired shortly after I came on, both of whom I was working for [in the first unit], and both of whom had different understandings about the nature of my job than the one I had originally negotiated. These were pretty high-powered people and that really affected my situation there. And so that was pretty unpleasant.

In addition to the discrepancy between the formal job description that Freda negotiated and the work she actually found herself doing, there was another major "unpleasant experience":

> Another thing I can recollect is that I enjoy doing research and there was someone I consulted with as a research person. This person was also transferred into the second unit I worked for and ended up doing the research project that I had originally consulted with him about. And that was again a part of the whole [unofficial] political arrangement there. Now that [too] was a very unpleasant experience.

According to Blau (1956) and Jacobs (1969), county civil service is often seen as the prototypical case of bureaucracy. The understanding is that it attempts to rationally order things for both staff and clients in such a way as to ensure the impartial distribution of services to clients and promotions and benefits to staff. Indeed, the civil service was established to ensure all of this and more (Gerth and Mills, 1946). However, due to what Blau calls "unofficial change" and what Jacobs terms "symbolic bureaucracy," rational and equitable upward mobility based on expertise and meritorious service is not always guaranteed. We have seen this repeatedly in the preceding case studies, which represent a wide range of bureaucratic work settings. The less than rational organization of the agency in question and its distribution of rewards and services has been repeatedly referred to by all of the professional women in this study as "politics" or "garbage." These two terms refer to the unequitable and/or irrational distribution of on-the-job rewards, the endless, meaningless "people work" necessary to cajole or "cool out" (Goffman, 1952) higher-echelon staff in an effort to circumvent uncalled for bureaucratic constraints, or the pointless formal formatting and/or wording of an endless stream of paperwork. "Politics," then, refers to the excessive rules and regulations that govern bureaucracies and was seen by the women in this study as the leading source of their frustration and burnout. It was also seen as the biggest impediment to their ability to do their jobs in an efficient and professional manner.

After thirteen years on the job, Freda experienced frustration and burnout. There was plenty of incentive to make a move to private practice, a change that would ultimately enhance her status, income, and job satisfaction. But, if there was plenty of incentive, initially there was little desire. Freda had insecurities of her own. First was her desire for economic security. The county job provided a good salary, benefits, and job security. Entering private practice, which Freda referred to quite rightly as "a business," was something she never felt quite comfortable with:

> I think it's very surprising to me that I'm in full-time private practice. I never would have considered myself a business person. And I think I'm still struggling to get a handle on that part of it. I think my prediction would have been that I would have been working for the county throughout my career.

There were other reasons why her desire for change was weak:

> I went into psychology because I wanted to help people. And I had all kinds of somewhat political idealistic feelings about that. The private sector seemed really unpopular in my thinking.

On a less idealistic and more immediate level, there was an apprehension and insecurity about entering the private sector. Freda never quite felt ready to risk private practice. First, there was the recognition that much of her higher education was irrelevant to the task at hand:

> Going into private practice has been complicated and difficult. I don't think my graduate education prepared me for a lot of the things you need to know and deal with as an independent businessperson.

Second, there was the economic and clinical insecurity of private practice. Finally, there was her early ambivalence toward the efficacy of psychology itself. She was never quite sure that it would benefit her patients.

> For many years I wasn't sure I believed in psychology. Maybe it's just a matter of getting to the point that I was sufficiently seasoned before I could tell that I was really helping people. And maybe it was finding the right theoretical persuasion. That made a big difference.

MOTIVATIONS AND INCENTIVES FOR CAREER CHANGE

While Freda has long since overcome her initial clinical and economic insecurities, they were nevertheless a prevalent part of her early career. Couple this with her political reservations, and all served as a powerful desire to maintain the status quo. We can see from her career path how slowly she waded in to test the waters, by spending seven years working half time in a clinic and half time in private practice, before jumping into a full-time private practice. All evidence points to Freda having a lifetime career as a county mental health psychologist. That she did not strongly suggests that in the absence of desire, there must have been a tremendous incentive to move Freda from the public to the private sector of clinical psychology. This incentive came from Freda's frustration and disenchantment with bureaucracy and its petty political games. We have seen in these case studies that not everyone has

the same burnout rate. Freda was able to contend with bureaucracy for thirteen years, while Fran was struggling after only one.
Ann, too, had a short fuse and exploded quickly. Joan took longer.
Notwithstanding their different tolerance levels, all of these
women experienced a sense of burnout that resulted primarily
from their encounters with bureaucracy, and it was this that ultimately catapulted them into upper-echelon administrative jobs or
into private practice. Although these moves did not provide the
perfect working environments either, they did provide higher
income, a sense of greater autonomy over their work, and enhanced status. With respect to lower frustration levels or higher
levels of job satisfaction, the move upward proved a mixed blessing. There was a certain nostalgia for the lower level, with the
more meaningful "people work" that the direct involvement with
the clients provided. Another plus of lower-level employment
was not only more meaningful people work, but less meaningless
paperwork. These were offset by the benefits of administrative
work noted above. The ambivalence this produced caused some
of the women in this study to seek the middle ground between the
pursuit of unbridled upward mobility and the stagnation of
lower-level positions.

THE WORK OF A PSYCHOLOGIST

As with the other professional women in this study, Freda had a
difficult time giving a detailed description of her work. After
repeated attempts she did describe what she did as a clinical psychologist in terms of who she saw, the nature of their problems,
their diagnostic categories, or her theoretical-clinical orientation. It
was impossible, however, to get her to address the second part of
the question—what she actually did while doing testing, play
therapy, or object relations therapy.

For example, when she included these clinical techniques
and/or theories in her practice, did she and her patients talk? If so,
was the talk in the form of an interview or naturally occurring
conversation (Schwartz and Jacobs, 1979)? Or, was it directive or
nondirective therapy? Who talked most? Who introduced topics
and guided the interview or conversation? Were the participants
seated, standing, or walking around when this occurred? During

play therapy with children, did Freda just observe the play or participate in it? How did she interpret what she saw the child doing
and on what basis? Did the children talk to her or she to them? If
so, how was this talk structured? What criteria or theoretical
framework did she use in order to interpret and assess the child's
behavior toward the toys or her? What assumptions did she make
about the child's actions in the office setting, and how did they
mirror those in outside settings? What basis existed for her believ-
ing these underlying assumptions on which the interpretations
and assessment were made? When testing children, how were the
tests administered to disruptive children who chose not to take
them? How did one interpret the results of the tests done to children who willingly participated versus those who reluctantly did
so, or those who refused to participate at all? What did Freda say
or do to get reluctant children to become willing participants?
What validity do the tests have and why does Freda think they are
valid, while other experts argue they are "culturally biased," or
that I.Q. refers only to one's performance on I.Q. tests? Freda was
unable to offer anything in an unsolicited way about what she did,
how she did it, and what she needed to know in order to be able to
do it. Despite repeated attempts, it was impossible to get her to
address these questions. Examples of these efforts will be offered
later in the chapter. Freda was, however, able to talk about what
she did on the job in terms of her abstract, general understanding
of the work; even if she offered very little concrete description.

Freda runs her private practice from a suite of offices that she
shares with other helping professionals—a psychiatrist, a social
worker, and a family counselor. While the first half of her career in
psychology was devoted to a children's practice focused primarily on testing and evaluation, her current caseload is divided
equally between adults and children and between testing and
therapy. Freda, in summarizing who she sees and why, describes
it this way:

> I guess I see adults who come to see me because they are
> troubled, they're confused, depressed or they're frightened.
> They're not in control of themselves or their lives and they
> come to talk to me about their concerns with the goal of
> developing more understanding of themselves, [to develop]

their ability to choose and direct what happens to themselves. I see them for fifty minutes and I talk to them.

And then I see children. I have a playroom and they and their parents come because they [the parents] are worried that their children are immature or have learning disorders or behavioral problems in school; children who are out of touch with themselves. Some are very shy. Some of them are very aggressive. When I see a child, that'll be a session which is usually primarily playing [play therapy], and their parents will come in for parent counseling, sometimes as a couple, sometimes the whole family. With child cases, I will have a certain amount of contact with people in schools . . . that kind of thing.

I: Can you give me some concrete examples of the kinds of problems your patients have?

Freda: Oh, people who are unable to work out relationships the way they want to, who find themselves breaking up with people they care about; people who feel like they don't know how to relax and enjoy their lives; people who are too pressured; people with drug problems who are out of control in that way; or people who are preoccupied with thoughts and ideas that torment them and they can't get control of their thinking or their fantasies; people who are depressed and lack confidence to accomplish the things they would like to in various ways. These would be examples.

I: Take any one of these problems, where people are depressed, or have unmanageable fantasies, or whatever. What do you do to help people with different sorts of problems? Is there one approach that's good for all problems or different approaches to different problems? How do you approach their problems and what do you actually do or say to help them?

Freda: I guess at the beginning there's clarification of just what it is that we're working on together. There's a definition of the ideas or directions that are not helpful or not realistic in various ways. And then there is an explanation of looking for reasons for this. I believe in the use of transference. I believe in the use of relationship. . . . I'm also currently very interested in the British Object Relations School.

I guess I used the developmental approach . . . it's very much relationship oriented. And, in the past I've been influenced by Freudian theory and also by Jungian theory and technique. I guess in my evaluation work [with the children] I use a very strong developmental and cognitive approach.

I: What do you do to help the children and how do you do it?

Freda: You have to come up with recommendations for remediation to improve their situations. You know, recommendations for how teachers can be more helpful in the classroom, maybe a different kind of school setting, certain kinds of tutoring, or remedial approaches. And also, possibly, psychotherapy, play therapy, family therapy or parent counseling. Those might all be recommendations. I think that summarizes it.

While Freda's responses offer a general overview of her practice—her patients, their problems, and her approach to them—they do not tell us in any concrete way what these theories and practices consist of. What does she actually say or do for the adults or children exhibiting the problems listed above? How do the different theoretical orientations she has held help her to understand or treat these problems? Why has she, over time, switched from one theoretical orientation and set of techniques to another, and how do these different theories and techniques result in different assessments, treatments, or understandings of her patients' problems?

To Freda, what was important in the account of her work was *what* she did and not *how* she did it. This was something she did not offer because it would have required that she be consciously aware of the routine, day-to-day practices of her work that made the job doable. It was this that resulted in her (and her peers' and patients') belief that she was a competent professional practitioner. The issue here is not whether Freda was or was not a competent clinical psychologist. The problem was that whether she and/or others thought she was or not, they were all incapable of telling why in terms of what Freda actually said or did to, with, or for her patients during their therapeutic encounters. This general inability to detail the day-to-day work practices that constituted their jobs was true of all the professional women in this study. We will now consider some allied aspects of work related to the private practice of clinical psychology. These support tasks, while not directly involved in therapy or evaluation, are nonetheless an essential part of conducting a practice.

THE PRACTICAL SIDE OF THE PRACTICE

As with Fran in the previous chapter, billing and the collection of bills in the conduct of her business was a major source of grief for Freda.

> I recently revised my system for billing and keeping track of money. Namely, I've gotten an IBM-clone computer system. And, what I try to do is at the end of every work day, I come home and type in who I saw and what charges there were for that day, and then the machine keeps track of it over the month. And that's made the billing much easier. And also, it's gotten rid of what I used to have to do previously, pay a bookkeeper, which has been a nice development. It was difficult to learn how to use it, but I'm gradually becoming more comfortable with it. That's been a huge relief.

In addition to the problem of direct billings and payments from patients, there was the problem of indirect billing and payments through insurance companies.

> Occasionally, issues come up with insurance companies. Like there's one new case now where the insurance company just approves of a small number of visits and it's very hard to understand what the procedures are to request additional visits. The people that you talk to in the insurance agency give you incorrect information, and that's time consuming and irritating.

These comments sound like Fran's experiences with the state bureaucracy while trying to get information on correct procedures for establishing a billing system. Freda, however, had an option for resolving the billing problem that Fran did not have.

I deal with that [the insurance company problem] by insisting that the patients have to take care of that and do it [handle the paperwork and any ensuing problems] themselves.

In addition to routine daily entries and dealing with insurance problems, Freda is confronted at the end of each month with another major investment of time and effort.

Freda: Then, of course, at the end of every month, there's a big time investment [needed] to get the records straight, actually printing up the bills, making sure they are correct, and getting them into the mail. That probably comes to six hours minimum. . . . Maybe you should add another hour or two. I have to deal with all those IPOs, IPAs, and PPOs. They're just proliferating.
I: What do those abbreviations mean?
Freda: These are managed health care arrangements. They're a whole new development in mental health now. And so, when you get a new one, there are all these forms you have to fill out. They're [the forms, rules, and regulations] always changing, and there's new forms to fill out. Or, you know, they'll send you statements, you pay dues, and so there are a lot of things that go on about that.
I: Before you got your computerized system and you had a bookkeeper, did you spend more or less time with billing?
Freda: When I used to type bills myself it was a nightmare. It was really unpleasant. . . . Then there is another issue which is the people who don't pay their bills. You have to go after them either on the phone, or in a couple of cases, I've had to get a collection agency. . . . I think it's getting better. I think I am having fewer of the real deadbeats than I used to. So it's not as big a problem [as it used to be].
I: Is there anything else you can think of?
Freda: There are other business issues. For example, occasionally I'll see someone on Medi-Cal. And that's a big hassle, dealing with them. They'll [the medical provider] deny payment, and the paperwork there is really unpleasant. It's getting worse.

Freda found that writing, serving, and collecting bills for her
service was only one frustrating and time-consuming aspect of the
practical trivial duties that her private practice required. Another
was keeping in touch with her patients.

> You know, another thing that I didn't think of before, is this
> whole issue of an answering service. I used to have an
> answering service which was costly and was also the origin
> of a lot of problems. And when I finally bit the bullet and
> made a decision to just have tapes [get an answering
> machine]. I feel as though that made life much easier and
> saved a lot of money.
>   You know, answering services make errors and generally
> speaking, they don't pay [their employees] a whole lot. The
> people who work there are highly pressured and dealing
> with crises. You know, if somebody's having a heart attack,
> that will get higher priority over your patient who is very
> needy and upset [this practice produced a time lag in her
> getting necessary information that was sometimes clinically
> upsetting]. You know, patients would complain about the
> answering service, or you would lose information that you
> needed and stuff like that.

Private practice has a number of other problems, some of them
social in nature. For example, working alone tends to isolate the
practitioner from others socially and professionally. This was
another practical problem Freda had to make a conscious effort to
contend with.

> One of the big problems with private practices is that you
> can feel isolated. And so, I make it a point to stay in touch
> with people. And I meet fairly regularly with people who are
> colleagues and friends of mine, where we talk about books,
> professional issues, and present cases to each other, so that I
> make sure that . . . I don't feel isolated.

In addition to these informal, unstructured get-togethers with colleagues and friends, Freda attends formal seminars in an effort to
keep abreast of her field of interest. She also attends professional

meetings, partially to keep in touch with developments in the field, and partially to find out about and influence issues related to politics and business.

Now, for example, this coming week I'll be on call for a week for the local psychiatry organization. And occasionally I'll go to meetings that they sponsor . . . and, I'll probably spend a lot of time at the meetings. And there's also various political kinds of investments in terms of promoting the future of psychology at large that's pretty important. For example, there was a recent Supreme Court decision that gave psychologists the right to admit people—patients—to inpatient mental health services. And so there are a lot of things going on to set that into motion. That's all pretty important . . . that will be a big change for psychology.

Some of the clinical and business features of Freda's work as a clinical psychologist in private practice have been outlined. We can see how her current professional involvements produced their ups and downs. But all things considered, Freda still prefers private practice to public service.

I: What are some of the differences between your current full-time private practice and your former work with the county?
Freda: The difference between working for the county and being in private practice?
I: Yeah.
Freda: Oh, I enjoy private practice a great deal more. It may be a timeline in my professional development. During the period I've been in full-time practice, I've begun to feel more seasoned and therefore more comfortable in doing the work. Therefore, I'm enjoying it more. It makes a big difference that you can do what you believe is the right thing to do, and you don't have other people who have a say [in what you do] for all kinds of reasons, the most unpleasant being budgetary constraints. You know, if the patient says "I can't afford to continue," you're in a position to negotiate it, if you want to. I also feel that my own development has grown a lot in pri-

vate practice, something I doubt would have happened if I continued for the county.

Further examples of the negative aspects of Freda's work with the county are given below:

When I was transferred from the first to the second unit, there were cases I was involved [with] which had to suddenly end. And that was very destructive clinically, and there was nothing [I] could do about it. . . . It's when something that's really clinically unfortunate happens, and you just don't have any control in the decision making [that it's bad].

Like you could be working collaboratively, that's done a lot, and all of a sudden, you're seeing a child and the mother's therapist is transferred to another part of the county. That can affect the whole case. And then there is the expectation that that might happen [even if it hasn't yet]. And that can affect everybody's morale. And who knows what effects it has on your own work. . . . The client has no control over that and neither do you. It's not a good feeling.

In addition to the political, budgetary, and general bureaucratic considerations that adversely affected her clinical practice, along with her morale and that of clients, there was the heavy caseload and endless paperwork that went with the county job.

Well, when you work for the county, there's pressure to keep your hours filled and see a large volume [of patients]. Although I think I was lucky. It's gotten much worse now. Those pressures are really unpleasant now. And the paperwork for the county has gotten much worse from what I hear. There was a certain amount of keeping track [of the patient's progress] that you had to do, writing summaries and things like that [that required less paperwork then than now]. But, that's really minimal in private practice.

Another practical problem associated with private practice was establishing a referral network. Success in this undertaking hinged on two major considerations: networking and personality. How well one succeeded depended in large part on one's personality. Freda told us that she was not very good at networking because she was not very outgoing.

I: Did you find it difficult to develop a private practice?
Freda: Oh . . . that's a sore issue because I'm not very outgoing. I have a lot of trouble making a strong promotional approach. And I think the practice has grown slowly because of this. I think that is probably a relevant issue [in the development of my practice]. I feel as though there are a number of people in the community who know my work and that's a continuing [and growing] thing. But I'm not one that can develop a referral source that's reliable. There are people who know how to do that [laughs], but that's not a skill I seem to have.

Notwithstanding her lack of promotional skills, Freda's practice is currently doing well. In fact, its success depends on another issue, unrelated to stable referral networks or an extroverted personality. It has to do with her idea of an optimal number of clients to satisfy clinical, financial, and leisure time requirements. One problem in establishing a private practice is having too few patients, resulting in financial insecurity. Working for the county took care of that by providing financial security and too many patients. Freda has to establish how many patients are necessary and how many constitute an overload.

I think people I know talk about that [how many patients to accept] as a difficult issue. The feeling is that either you have too few or too many. I feel comfortable with it financially now [the number of patients] but, you know, who knows what could happen. I have not yet developed a way that I feel is good or effective [in] dealing with the issue of too much or how many is good. I find myself tired and I don't know whether that's because the practice is too full, or if it's because I don't distribute my time in the best way. That's confusing. . . . I haven't quite got that established for myself as well as I would like.

In examining the work of a clinical psychologist in public and private practice, we have seen how some of this work has little if anything to do with therapy and/or testing. A fair amount of it, with respect to private practice, has to do with the practical problems of running any business. This was even more the case with clinical psychologists in public practice. In fact, when all of the trivial and nonessential aspects of the work of the professional women in this study is viewed collectively, we can see that these activities comprised a nontrivial proportion of their everyday work time and, that in terms of the time, effort, and grief it took to accomplish these routine activities, there was nothing trivial about them at all. Indeed, they were very substantial.

In this sense, we have been dealing in different ways and contexts with the nontrivial nature of trivia. These activities include all sorts of routine tasks people do on the job from making coffee, sharpening pencils, "shooting the breeze," having a snack, hunting for information, holding office birthday parties, having a smoke, and many other duties that do not appear either as a part of the formal written job description or in workers' accounts of what they do on the job. All of these informal activities are as much a part of the job as the formal features of the job found in the official job description. Also, a part of the job are those things that workers routinely do that deal directly with the work at hand but are not a part of the job description. These case studies, taken collectively, display some of the essential, informal, and unofficial accomplishments of work. Finally, these case studies reveal the circuitous and fortuitous route by which these professional women came to their professions. It also describes the work they actually did, and to a lesser extent, how they succeeded in doing it.

8

Summary and Conclusions

This book offered a detailed case study analysis of the employment careers of several professional women, out of which sprang a number of work-related issues. While these women were able to describe in a general way the kind of work they did, they had trouble describing in any detail the concrete features of that work—what they actually did to accomplish the jobs they described. We have dealt with why this form of description was so difficult, if not impossible. This led to a discussion of the non-trivial nature of trivia in work settings, and why so much of their work entailed politics, "garbage," and other forms of unproductive, annoying, and trivial tasks. We have seen how, when viewed collectively, these trivial tasks constituted a substantial part of the real work they routinely did. We have also seen how they failed to subvert the workings of "the system" in an effort to minimize or eliminate this garbage from their work-a-day world.

These women also lived with the ubiquitous effects of trivia on the pre-conscious or unconscious level of the taken-for-granted or tacitly understood. Here there was no need to consciously confront the effects of trivia since at this level they were unable to "see" or "know" it, and it posed no practical work-related problem for them. This study was least successful in revealing the nontrivial nature of trivia at this level because the only access to this form of trivia was through the workers' accounts of it, which they could not give, since they had no conscious awareness of it. A better understanding of trivia at this level required the detailed descriptions of work over prolonged periods of time by talented participant-observers. This sort of data is sorely lacking. Even on the rare occasion that the detailed descriptions of actual work practices are available, they are usually analyzed by researchers with different agendas than those proposed here. It is not only laypeople but also social science researchers who have shown little interest in the nontrivial nature of trivia in everyday life.

The negative effects of bureaucratic forms of organization in a variety of work settings have also been addressed. This study showed the ingenious ways that workers tried to subvert, circumvent, or abolish the counterproductive and demoralizing effects of bureaucratic constraints. For those who were confronted by the "regs" day-in and day-out, year after year, and still hoped to take some pride in their work, this took a heroic effort.

We have seen how in every case the professional women in this study were confronted with the discrepancy between what they expected their job to entail, and the work they actually did. Many of the women were also surprised to find that their extensive formal education had little if anything to do with certain important aspects of their work. These essential skills had to be acquired informally through hands-on experience and on-the-job training. Finally, we saw how the meaning of work resided less in one's salary, benefits, or hours worked, than in the positive interactions workers were able to establish between themselves, their employers, their peers, and their clients.

This study did not deal with professional men at work. Much of what has been said here, however, about the experience of professional women working in bureaucratic settings applies equally to men. The bureaucratic problems these women confronted should not be seen as gender related, as much as systemic. As Weber astutely noted, the officeholder at any level of bureaucracy, be it a man or a woman, is likely to suffer the problem of being reduced to the lowest possible denominator. Bureaucracies have no place for the "virtuoso" or "charismatic man" (or woman) (Gerth and Mills, 1946).

Another topic not addressed here was the lack of upward mobility of women doing the same work as men. That women are generally discriminated against in the workplace, and ought not to be, was accepted as a given. It was not discussed here because of the wealth of information on this topic and also because only one of the professional women interviewed brought up the topic of work discrimination in a single passing reference. None mentioned the issue of sexual harassment. Each of these taped interviews was about one and a half hours long and produced a transcript that was an average of 50 double-spaced pages in length. This resulted in a total of 250–300 pages of transcript. Since the topics of work discrimination and/or sexual harassment did not emerge naturally from the data, there was no compelling reason to treat them within the context of this study. In fact, most of the work-related problems that the women in this study had were with other women, since, in most cases, their bosses were women.

The attempted escape from the ubiquitous effects of trivia in our everyday life (Cohen and Taylor, 1978; Jacobs, 1989) is not restricted to ordinary people. Even geniuses who undertook this gargantuan task were doomed to failure. A dramatic example of this failure is shown in Van Gogh's letters to his brother Theo (Stone, 1969). These were largely devoted to problems of the minutiae of everyday life. Year after year, these letters spoke poignantly of Van Gogh's valiant efforts to pay the rent; sell a painting; buy food, paint, or canvas; or not be harassed by the provincial townsfolk for being different. His only wish was to make a living at painting, have some meager shelter, work at his chosen profession, and be left in peace. Few of us seem to be able to manage this. A *New Yorker* cartoon I came across a few years ago recognized the universality of the problem. It showed a little boy in lederhosen, with a lot of hair, playing the piano with gusto. In the doorway, watching him with arms akimbo, was a large hausfrau hollering, "Ludwig! The garbage!" And so it seems that no matter how hard we try we are all destined to deal with the garbage of everyday life.

Bibliography

Ayalti, J., ed. 1971. *Yiddish Proverbs*. New York: Shocken Books.

Becker, Howard. 1973. *Outsiders: Studies in the Sociology of Deviance*. Rev. ed. New York: Free Press.

——, ed. 1981. *Exploring Society Photographically*. Evanston, IL: Northwestern University Press.

Becker, H. S., et al. 1961. *Boys in White*. Chicago: University of Chicago Press.

Blau, Peter M. 1956. *Bureaucracy in Modern Society*. New York: Random House.

Brautigan, Richard. 1972. "The Pretty Office." In *Revenge of the Lawn: Stories 1962–1970*. New York: Pocket Books.

Braverman, Harry. 1974. *Labor and Monopoly Capital: The Degradation of Work in the Twentieth Century*. New York: Monthly Review Press.

Cantor, Kenneth P., et al. 1988. "Hair Dye Use and Risk of Leukemia and Lymphoma." *American Journal of Public Health* 78,5:570–71.

Cohen, Michelle, Jean-Yves Jaffray, and Tanios Said. 1987. "Experimental Comparison of Individual Behavior Under Risk and Under Uncertainty for Gains and for Losses." *Organizational Behavior and Human Decision Processes* 39:1–22.

Cohen, Stanley, and Laurie Taylor. 1978. *Escape Attempts: The Theory and Practice of Resistance in Everyday Life*. New York: Penguin Books.

Crawford, S. 1989. *Technical Workers in an Advanced Society*. New York: Cambridge University Press.

Dalton, Melville. 1966. *Men Who Manage*. New York: John Wiley & Sons.

Davis, Harold, Patricia A. Honchar, and Lucina Suarez. 1987. "Fatal Occu-
    pational Injuries of Women, Texas 1975–1984." *American Journal of
    Public Health* 77,12:1524–27.
Ekman, Paul. 1965. "Communication Through Nonverbal Behavior: A
    Source of Information About Interpersonal Relationships." In
    Affect, Cognition, and Personality, eds. S. Tomkins and C. Izard,
    390–442. New York: Springer Publishing Co.
Emerson, Joan P. 1970. "Nothing Unusual Is Happening." In *Human
    Nature and Collective Behavior*, ed. Tamotsu Shibutani. Englewood
    Cliffs, NJ: Prentice-Hall.
Fagley, N. S., and Paul M. Miller. 1987. "The Effects of Decision-Framing
    on Choice of Risky vs. Certain Options." *Organizational Behavior
    and Human Decision Processes* 39:264–77.
Frank, Robert H. 1988. *Passions Within Reason*. New York: W. W. Norton.
Friedland, William H., and Dorothy Nelkin. 1971. *Migrant: Agricultural
    Workers in America's Northeast*. New York: Holt, Rinehart and
    Winston.
Garfinkel, L. 1984. "Cigarette Smoking and Coronary Heart Disease in
    Blacks: Comparison to Whites in a Prospective Study." *American
    Heart Journal* 108:802–7.
Garfinkle, Harold. 1967. *Studies in Ethnomethodology*. Englewood Cliffs,
    NJ: Prentice-Hall.
Garson, Barbara. 1977. *All the Live Long Day: The Meaning and Demeaning
    of Routine Work*. New York: Penguin Books.
———. 1988. *The Electronic Sweatshop: How Computers Are Transforming the
    Office of the Future into the Factory of the Past*. New York: Simon and
    Schuster.
Gerth, H. H., and C. Wright Mills, eds. and trans. 1946. *From Max Weber:
    Essays in Sociology*. New York: Oxford University Press, 215.
Giddings, Franklin H. 1896. *The Principles of Sociology: An Analysis of the
    Phenomena of Association and Social Organization*. New York:
    Macmillan.
Goffman, Erving. 1952. "On Cooling the Mark Out: Some Aspects of
    Adaptation to Failure." *Psychiatry* 15: 451–63.
———. 1959. *The Presentation of Self in Everyday Life*. Garden City, NY:
    Doubleday/Anchor.
———. 1979. *Gender Advertisement*. New York: Harper & Row.
Greenhouse, Steven. 1992. "The Coming Crisis of the American Work-
    force." *New York Times*, June 7, 14f.
Gubrium, Jaber F. 1975. *Living and Dying in Murray Manor*. New York: St.
    Martin's.
Harper, Douglas. 1990. Review of *Images of History: Nineteenth and Early*

Twentieth Century Latin American Photographs as Documents by Robert M. Levine. *Contemporary Sociology* 19, 2 (March).

Hertz, David B., and Howard Thomas. 1983. *Risk Analysis and Its Applications*. New York: John Wiley & Sons.

Hochschild, Arlie Russell. 1983. *The Managed Heart: Commercialization of Human Feeling*. Berkeley, CA: The University of California Press.

Hudson, Randy. 1991. "The Active Worker: Compliance and Autonomy at the Workplace." *Journal of Contemporary Ethnography* 20, 1: 47–78.

Jacobs, Jerry. 1969. " 'Symbolic Bureaucracy': A Case Study of a Social Welfare Agency." *Social Forces* 47, 4: 413–22.

———. 1971. "From Sacred to Secular: The Rationalization of Christian Theology." *Journal for the Scientific Study of Religion* 10, 1: 151–57.

———. 1974. *Fun City: An Ethnographic Study of Retirement Community*. New York: Holt, Rinehart and Winston.

———. 1982. *In the Best Interest of the Child: An Evaluation of Assessment Centers*. Oxford: Pergamon Press.

———. 1982. *The Search for Help: A Study of the Retarded Child in the Community*. Lanham, MD: University Press of America.

———. 1989. *The Search for Acceptance: Consumerism, Sexuality, and Self Among American Women*. Bristol, IN: Wyndham Hall Press.

Jacobs, Jerry, and Barry Glassner. 1982. "Manic Depression and Suicide." *Case Analysis* 2,1.

James, P. D. 1989. *Shroud for a Nightingale*. London: Penguin Books.

Johnson, John M. 1975. *Doing Field Research*. New York: The Free Press.

Jones, Frank E. 1984. "Reflections on Work Organization Among Structural Steelworkers." In *The Sociology of Work: Papers in Honour of Oswald Hall*, ed. Audrey Wipper. Ottawa, Canada: Carleton University Press.

Karasek, Robert A., et al. 1988. "Job Characteristics in Relation to the Prevalence of Myocardial Infarction in the US Health Examination Survey (HES) and the Health Nutrition Examination Survey (HANES)." *American Journal of Public Health* 78,8:910–18.

Lakoff, Robin T., and Raquel L. Scheer. 1984. *Face Value: The Politics of Beauty*. New York: Routledge Chapman & Hall.

Levin, Irwin P., Mary A. Snyder, and Daniel P. Chapman. 1988. "The Interaction of Experiential and Situational Factors and Gender in a Simulated Risky Decision-Making Task." *Journal of Psychology* 122:173–81.

MacCrimmon, Kenneth R., and Donald Wehrung. 1986. *Taking Risks: The Management of Uncertainty*. New York: The Free Press.

Matza, David. 1964. *Delinquency and Drift*. New York: John Wiley & Sons.

Merton, Robert K. 1957. *Social Theory and Social Structure*. rev. ed. Glencoe, IL: Free Press.

Mills, C. Wright. 1956. *White Collar: The American Middle Classes*. New York: Oxford University Press.

Occupational Safety and Health Administration (OSHA). January 14, 1983. "Occupational Exposure to Inorganic Arsenate." *Federal Register* 48:1864–1903.

Orwell, George. 1933. *Down and Out in Paris and London*. New York: Harcourt Brace Jovanovich.

Pfuhl, Erdwin H., Jr. 1986. *The Deviance Process*. 2nd ed. Belmont, CA: Wadsworth.

Pike, Royston E. 1972. *Golden Times: Human Documents of the Victorian Age*. New York: Shocken Books.

Ponte, Meredith R. 1974. "Driving Is a Privilege: License Among Licensers." In *Deviance: Field Studies and Self-Disclosures*, ed. Jerry Jacobs. Palo Alto, CA: Mayfield.

Radner, Gilda. 1990. *It's Always Something*. New York: Avon Books.

Rinsland, H. D. 1990. *The Basic Vocabulary of Elementary School Children*. New York: Macmillan.

Schutz, Alfred. 1967. *The Phenomenology of the Social World*. Evanston, IL: Northwestern University Press.

Schwartz, Howard, and Jerry Jacobs. 1979. *Qualitative Sociology: A Method to the Madness*. New York: The Free Press.

Seeman, Melvin. 1959. "On the Meaning of Alienation." *American Sociological Review* 24 (December): 783–91.

Simmel, Georg. 1950. "The Metropolis and Mental Life." In *The Sociology of Georg Simmel*, trans. and ed. Kurt H. Wolff. Glencoe, IL: Free Press.

Stein, Howard S., and Ian S. Jones. 1988. "Crash Involvement of Large Trucks by Configuration: A Case Control Study." *American Journal of Public Health* 78,5:491–98.

Steinbeck, John. 1986. *The Log from the Sea of Cortez*. New York: Penguin Books.

Steufert, Siegfried. 1986. "Individual Differences in Risk Taking." *Journal of Applied Social Psychology* 16,6:482–97.

Stone, Irving. 1969. *Dear Theo*. New York: New American Library.

Tart, Charles T. 1972. "States of Consciousness and State-Specific Sciences." *Science* 176:1203–10.

Teta, M. J., et al. 1984. "Cancer Incidence Among Cosmetologists." *Journal of National Cancer Institute* 72:1051–57.

Thomas, W. I., and Florian Znaniecki. 1928. *The Child in America*. New York: Alfred A. Knopf.

Twain, Mark. 1958. *The Complete Short Stories of Mark Twain*, ed. Charles
    Neider. New York: Bantam Books.
Ute, Grante. 1974. "One, Two, Three, Red Light: Judicial Review in a Traf-
    fic Court." In *Deviance: Field Studies and Self-Disclosures*, ed. Jerry
    Jacobs. Palo Alto, CA: Mayfield.
Weber, Max. 1958. *The Protestant Ethic and Spirit of Capitalism*. New York:
    Scribners.
Wolfe, Tom. 1987. *The Bonfire of the Vanities*. New York: Bantam Books.

Index

About the Author

JERRY JACOBS is Professor Emeritus of Sociology at Syracuse University and author of thirteen books, including *Fun City* (1974, 1978, 1983), *The Moral Justification of Suicide* (1982), and *The Mall: An Attempted Escape from Everyday Life* (1984).